Correspondences

Correspondences

Tim Ingold

polity

Internal branch images: Insh1na/iStock

First published in 2021 by Polity Press

Polity Press
65 Bridge Street
Cambridge CB2 1UR, UK

Polity Press
101 Station Landing
Suite 300
Medford, MA 02155, USA

ISBN-13: 978-1-5095-4410-3
ISBN-13: 978-1-5095-4411-0 (pb)

A catalogue record for this book is available from the British Library.

Typeset in 9.5 on 14 Fournier by Servis Filmsetting Ltd, Stockport, Cheshire
Printed and bound in Great Britain by TJ International Limited

The publisher has used its best endeavours to ensure that the URLs for external
websites referred to in this book are correct and active at the time of going to
press. However, the publisher has no responsibility for the websites and can make
no guarantee that a site will remain live or that the content is or will remain
appropriate.

Every effort has been made to trace all copyright holders, but if any have been
overlooked the publisher will be pleased to include any necessary credits in any
subsequent reprint or edition.

For further information on Polity, visit our website: politybooks.com

Contents

Preface and acknowledgements

Over the years I have made a habit of composing letters. Unaddressed, they have entered my notebook in the form of responses to things I have come across which have roused my curiosity. These things, however, never ceased to prey on my mind, nor did I cease to ponder them. It is as if we had embarked on a kind of correspondence. In this book, I open a collection of such curious correspondences. Nearly all began, for me, during the past decade, and most within the five years between 2013 and 2018. These were the years in which I was preoccupied with leading a large project, funded by the European Research Council, entitled *Knowing From the Inside* (or KFI, for short). The aim of the project was to forge a different way of thinking about how we come to know things: not through engineering a confrontation between theories in the head and facts on the ground, but rather through corresponding with the things themselves, in the very processes of thought.

The essays assembled here all exemplify this aim in one way or another, and they range over the four fields that the KFI project sought to harness to it: of anthropology, art, architecture and design. An earlier version of the book, with just sixteen chapters (including four essays and three interviews omitted from the new version), was published 'in house' by the University of Aberdeen, in 2017, as one of a series of experimental volumes resulting from the project.[1] Although I have carried over nine essays from the original version into the new one, several of them have been revised, and others are almost completely rewritten. The remaining eighteen essays are new material.

I owe an immense debt of gratitude to everyone in the KFI project for their inspiration and support, and to the European Research Council for the funding that made it all possible. In addition I have many individuals to thank, both for inspiration and for allowing the reuse of previously published material. They are: Anaïs Tondeur, Anna Macdonald, Anne Dressen, Anne Masson, Benjamin Grillon, Bob Simpson, Carol Bove, Claudia Zeiske and Deveron Arts, Colin Davidson, David Nash, Émile Kirsch, Eric Chevalier, Franck Billé, Germain Meulemans, Giuseppe Penone, Hélène Studievic, Kenneth Olwig, Marie-Andrée Jacob, Mathilde Roussel, Matthieu Raffard, Michael Malay, Mikel Nieto, Nisha Keshav, Philip Vannini, Rachel Harkness, Robin Humphrey, Shauna McMullan, Tatum Hands, Tehching Hsieh, Tim Knowles, Tomás Saraceno and Wolfgang Weileder. My gratitude to all. This book could not have been completed without you!

'Somewhere in Northern Karelia . . .' is reproduced by courtesy of Penguin Random House; 'In the shadow of tree being' by courtesy of the Gagosian Gallery; 'On flight' by courtesy of Skira Editore; 'Words to meet the world' and 'Diabolism and logophilia' by courtesy of Routledge (Taylor & Francis).

Tim Ingold
Aberdeen, March 2020

Invitation

Letters from the heart

Ideas come when you least expect them. If a thought were an expected visitor to your mind, and came knocking by appointment, would it even be an idea at all? For the thought to be an idea it has to disturb, to unsettle, like a gust of wind ruffling through a heap of leaves. You may have been waiting for it, but it still comes as a surprise. Those, however, who aim to get from A to B as quickly as possible have no time to wait. For them, the idea is an unwelcome guest, threatening to throw them off course, if not with losing their way altogether. Yet were it not for ideas, we'd be trapped. The life of the mind would be confined to a shuffle, where nothing really new could ever arise, only rearrangements of an existing pack. These days it has become usual to think of creativity like that: to suppose that there is no new idea that is not a novel permutation or combination of the fragments of old ones. It is as though the mind were a kaleidoscope, equipped with a fixed structure of mirrors and an assortment of beads of different shapes and colours. The mirrors are hardwired cognitive structures, the beads their mental content. Every shake yields a unique pattern, but while we celebrate its novelty, nothing new comes out of it. Each is an end in itself; there is no beginning. Unless . . . unless we attend to what is usually forgotten, the shake itself. The shake unsettles, there is a momentary loosening, a loss of control. What if the idea were the shake, rather than the pattern that results from it?

'I'm all shook up,' sang Elvis Presley; 'my hands are shaky and my knees are weak.' Elvis was in love, but I've experienced the same nervous agitation when unexpectedly overtaken by an idea. It is as visceral as it is intellectual, if the two can be distinguished at all. The thinker may sometimes seem detached, head in hands, isolated in a bubble, but the lover's pose is much the same. What the thinker and the lover have in common is that they are uniquely vulnerable. They are in a condition of surrender, whether to the idea or to the beloved. But the condition is far from passive; on the contrary, it is passionate, an affectation of the soul that calls mind and body to contemplation that is furious in its intensity. And it is the fury of thinking, not just in anger but in ecstasy, that I want to celebrate in these pages. It is a fury, in my experience, that can be endured only in relative quietude, when all around is in a moderate state of balance. In the contemporary world, such balance is hard to find, and all the more precious because of it. My fear is that the imbalances of the world – of wealth, climate and education – will render thinking unsustainable, and jeopardize the life of the mind. Indeed we are faced with an epidemic of thoughtlessness, the root causes of which lie in the evacuation from thought of any consideration for its consequences, as if to think were no longer even to care, let alone to love.

It is left for us to decide, warned the philosopher Hannah Arendt, 'whether we love the world enough to assume responsibility for it'.[1] Arendt was writing in the wake of the destruction of the Second World War, but with the world once again on a knife-edge, her words carry equal force today. Only if we fall back in love with the world, she foretold, can there be hope of renewal for generations to come. And to do that, we need to relearn the art of thinking, and of writing, from the heart as much as from the head. In the past, we would think and write like this especially when scribing letters to loved ones, family and friends. As we set pen to paper, our thoughts would fly to the intended recipient, as though we were together with them in conversation. We used to write as we would speak, with feeling and concern, not to publicize a thesis but to carry on a line of thinking that responds, in its moods and motivations, to what we suppose might be going through the mind of the addressee. Working things out as we go along, ideas would appear here with a certain freshness and spontaneity, not yet weighed down by the burdens of subsequent elaboration. But with letter-writing it is not only the words we select that matter; it is also how we write them. Words written by hand, in a cursive script, convey feeling in the very gravity and inflection of the continually looping letter-line. This is more than words can say, yet words are saying it, not by way of the meanings we ascribe to them, but thanks to the expressive power of the line itself. You know me, and how I feel, from the way I write, just as you do from my voice. Everyone's way is different.

Digitization and loss

Nowadays, this kind of letter-writing has all but ceased, to be replaced by the instant communication of phone and email. And with that, something of the care and spontaneity of letter-writing has been lost. Or, more to the point, the spontaneity of communication, since it is over in an instant, has become careless, stripped of the attention and deliberation that goes into fashioning lines on the page, in writing, and of the patience entailed in waiting: for the letter to reach its intended destination, and for the response to come back from the recipient. Conversely, care has lost much of its spontaneity: it seems more calculated and, by the same token, less personal, less imbued with feeling. It has become a service to be delivered rather than a recognition, in attention and response, of what we owe to others for our own existence as beings in a world. Now some might say that it is merely nostalgic to attempt to bring care and spontaneity back together again. I disagree, however, and I offer this book both as an example of how this can be done, and as a testament to the power of written correspondence in achieving it. For it is not a matter of going back into the past; it is rather about allowing the past once more to feel its way into the future. For life on earth to carry on, and to flourish, we need to learn to attend to the world around us, and to respond with sensitivity and judgement. Corresponding with people and things – as we used to do in letter-writing – opens paths for lives to carry on, each in its own way but nevertheless with regard for others.

In this book, I have compiled some of the ways I have personally corresponded, in writing, with everything from oceans and skies, and from landscapes and forests, to monuments and artworks. Ideally, I should have written these correspondences by hand. That I have written them on a keyboard is, for me, a shortcoming; that you should be reading them in print unfortunate. This regret is not a retreat into nostalgia, however, but a plea for sustainability. A world in which every communication is over almost before it begins, reducing life to a succession of instants, is simply not sustainable. Nor is it nostalgic to wish to preserve our capacities for humane expression. For we lose these powers at our peril. Never in human history, indeed, have they been at greater risk. We have stood by as words, severed from hand and mouth, have been converted into the liquid currency of a global information and communications industry. In hock to states and corporations, words have been reduced to mere tokens of exchange. And our technologies have evolved in step. Language has been distilled from the conversations of life, only to be inserted into the mechanisms of computation. Yet the much-vaunted 'digital revolution' will almost certainly self-destruct, probably within this century. In a world facing climate emergency, it too is manifestly unsustainable. Not only are the supercomputers on which it depends already consuming colossal quantities of energy; the extraction of toxic heavy metals for use in digital devices has also fuelled genocidal conflict around the world, and will likely render many environments permanently uninhabitable. Meanwhile, digitization continues to dissolve the archives of recorded history at an unprecedented rate.

Imagine a future in which all written words are tapped out, on keyboards or screens. To read these words requires a vision that cuts through paper or glass, in order to extract the meanings reflected from behind, rather than allowing itself to be detained at the surface. The linear traces of affect, which had once captivated the eyes of readers, are now written off as a distraction. They have been replaced by a vocabulary of emoticons, presenting surrogates for feeling rather than feeling in itself. With the expressive power of the line long forgotten, next to go will be the voice. The authorities have decreed that the musical qualities of vocal pronunciation, which had once so enchanted listeners as to lure them to follow along, or even join in, are held to distract from what is now believed to be the proper function of words, to convey information. So the voice is to be replaced by digital synthesizers, operated by neurotransmitters from the brain. In this brave new world, the lullaby, the lament, the carol and the hum, eviscerated of affect, are to be preserved in aspic, as mementos of a bygone past. Deprived of voice, people lose the capacity to sing. But this only compounds the earlier suppression of the hand, in the loss of its capacity to write. A society without handwriting is like one from which song has been banished. Yet it would take only a simple invention to bring it back: a hand-held tube, fitted with a tip and filled with dark-hued liquid. No digital interface can match the expressive potential and versatility of this instrument. Cheap, easy to use, requiring no external power supply, and leaving no pollution in its wake, it could secure the future of writing for countless years to come.

More than human

I sometimes wonder where philosophers have been, all these years. Some of their number have recently taken to telling us – as though it were a startling new discovery – that the world does not actually revolve around human beings, and that non-human entities of all sorts can enter into relations with one another, and even hold meanings for one another, which do not depend in the slightest on how they are used or perceived by humans, or even on any human presence at all. The fact that researchers in such fields as plant and animal ecology, geomorphology and soil science have been studying such relations for generations seems to have passed our philosophers by. Of course we have good reason to question the premises that underpin such scientific endeavours. For the most part they assume that the world of nature already exists 'out there', like an unmapped continent, and is simply waiting for us humans to discover it. There is certainly something duplicitous about the claims of science to account for the workings of nature, including the mind as part of nature, given that such claims derive their authority from the sovereign perspective of a mind that has already set itself on a pedestal, over and above the nature it purports to explain. That's why, despite denials that for *any* species there exists an essence of its kind, science cannot escape the assumption that there is something exceptional about humans – something that lifts them up and over the natural world. It cannot escape this assumption because the entire scientific project depends on it. It's the elephant in the room, invisibly presiding over the science of non-human conviviality, amidst disavowals of its presence and influence.

But philosophers who call for a more balanced or 'symmetrical' approach, which would allow the participation of non-humans with humans on a level playing field, are no less two-faced. We humans, they say, are not in a world of our own. To the contrary, we share our world with an almost unimaginable variety of non-human kinds, forming relationships with and among them that ramify through ever-extending networks of influence and agency. And yet, at the centre of any network, you will always find a human. Why? Because human beings, according to those who take this view, are unique among living creatures in the extent to which they have the capacity to enrol other kinds into their own lifeways. They do so in their extensive use of inanimate objects as tools or for the manufacture of artefacts, in the domestication of plants and animals to suit their purposes, and through sundry other interventions. Thus humankind is posited as the pivot around which the balance of the human and the non-human turns. Yet the pivot is itself founded in one of the most potent myths of modernity. It is the myth of how, many millennia ago, the distant ancestors of modern-day humans broke the bonds of nature that hold all other animals captive, and launched themselves on the path of history. Paradoxically, an approach which purports to dismantle the distinction between the human and the non-human, and to level the playing field, is justified on the grounds that in their manner of engagement with material things, and in the progressive history of that engagement, human beings are radically distinct from all other living kinds. Hardly could a symmetrical approach rest on a more asymmetrical foundation![2]

The truth is that in a more-than-human world, nothing exists in isolation. Humans may share this world with non-humans, but by the same token, stones share it with non-stones, trees with non-trees and mountains with non-mountains. Yet where the stone ends and its contrary begins cannot be ascertained with any finality. The same goes for the tree and the mountain, even for the human. It is a condition of life that everything leaks, and nothing is locked in. Of course we can tell things apart. Ask me to point to another human being, or to a stone, a tree or a mountain, and I can readily do so. But what I'm pointing to is not an entity that is in any sense self-contained. My attention is rather directed towards a place from which I see something happening, a going-on that spills out into its surroundings, including myself. I see the stone in its stoning, the tree in its arborescence, the mountain in its rising and falling. Even a fellow human being I see in his or her humaning. We should replace our nouns for naming things with verbs: 'to stone', 'to tree', 'to mountain', 'to human'. At once the world we inhabit, and that we share with so many other things, no longer appears ready-cut, into things of this sort or that, along the lines of a classification. Instead we find ourselves pitched into a world in which things are ever-differentiating from one another along the folds and creases of their formation. Everything has – or, better, *is* – the story of its differentiation. Thus the story of a stone, a tree or a mountain, like the story of a human being, is also the story of those things or beings that, over time, become other to it – the moss, the bird, the mountaineer.

Being and becoming

Only when we appreciate things as their stories can we begin to correspond with them. So you, the reader, should practise this way of seeing before embarking upon the following essays. We are so used to taking a rearward view, to capturing things a moment too late, when they have already settled into the shapes and categories assigned to them. As in the game of grandmother's footsteps, the world creeps up on us behind our backs, but freezes on the instant when we turn around to look. To correspond we need to go behind the scenes, to join with the creepers and to move along with them in real time.

Immediately upon doing so, what grandmother sees only as statues come vibrantly to life. The statue is already cast, but the creepers are alive in the casting. Theirs is a stance not of being but of becoming. Corresponding with them calls for a shift, as philosophers would say, from ontology to ontogeny. Ontology is about what it takes for a thing to exist, but ontogeny is about how it is generated, about its growth and formation. This shift, moreover, has important ethical implications. For it suggests that things are far from closed to one another, each wrapped up in its own, ultimately impenetrable world of being. On the contrary, they are fundamentally open, and all participate in one indivisible world of becoming. Multiple ontologies signify multiple worlds, but multiple ontogenies signify one world. Since, in their growth or movement, the things of this world respond to one another, they are also responsible. And in this one world of ours, responsibility is not for some but not others. It is a burden that all must carry.

Now there are some who can only comprehend a way of thinking by first assigning it to a school of thought. And from what I've said so far, they would probably guess that I was schooled in phenomenology. It's perfectly true that I have been influenced by thinkers identified with this tradition. Yet phenomenology has not, for me, been a point of departure. I have never thought of it as an approach or way of working that I might first absorb and then apply. Like most things philosophical, it has grown on me more or less serendipitously, and has wormed its way into my thinking without my really noticing it. No doubt, this home-grown phenomenology of mine takes all kinds of liberties with the canonical texts, many of which I am happy to leave unread. Textual exegesis is a task for trained philosophers, and not for amateurs like me. I have always been slightly bemused by scholars who bury their heads in the most arcane and impenetrable of texts in the effort, they tell us, to get to the bottom of our experience as beings in a world. You would think that the best way to fathom the depths of human experience would be to attend to the world itself, and to learn directly from what it has to tell us. This is what inhabitants do all the time, in their daily lives, and we have much to learn from them. That's why I continue to insist that if we are even to begin to resolve the crisis in our habitation of the world, then we should listen to the wisdom of inhabitants, whether they be humans or beings of other kinds, rather than taking shelter in the closeted self-referentiality of philosophical discourse.

If, today, our world is in crisis, it is because we have forgotten how to correspond. We have engaged, instead, in campaigns of inter-action. Parties to interaction face each other with their identities and objectives already in place, and transact in ways that serve, but do nothing to transform, their separate interests. Their difference is given from the start, and remains afterwards. Interaction is thus a *between* relation. Correspondence, however, goes *along*. The trouble is that we have been so wrapped up in our interactions with others that we have failed to notice how both we and they go along together in the current of time. As I've tried to show, correspondence is about the ways along which lives, in their perpetual unfolding or becoming, simultaneously join together and differentiate themselves, one from another. This shift from interaction to correspondence entails a fun-damental reorientation, from the between-ness of beings and things to their *in-between-ness*.[3] Think of a river and its banks. We might speak of the relation of one bank to the other and, crossing a bridge, we might find ourselves halfway between the two. But the banks are perpetually forming and re-forming as the river waters sweep by. These waters flow in-between the banks, in a direction orthogonal to the span of the bridge. To say of beings and things that they are in-between is to align our awareness with the waters; to correspond with them is to join this awareness with the flow. Just such a shift of orientation is needed, I believe, if we are to understand the world as one that we can inhabit both now and for the foreseeable future. It is, in short, a condition for sustainable living.

A waste of knowing

All knowledge is crap: the waste product of a metabolic reaction. That, at any rate, is the conclusion which inevitably follows from the model of knowledge production imposed by our masters, whether they be educational institutions, business corporations or agents of the state. According to this model, knowledge is produced by harvesting quantities of data, and feeding it into machines that digest or process this 'input' and excrete the results, also known as 'output', at the other end. This excrement is the marketable currency of the knowledge economy. To the extent that human beings are involved at all in the productive process, they are but operators or technicians, there to serve the machines: to keep them supplied and in working order. Ideally, their presence and activity – beyond ensuring that the machines work – should have no bearing on the results. Inputs go in, outputs come out, what happens in-between is of no particular consequence. And as the results pile up, and the excremental heaps of knowledge relentlessly swell, life itself is consigned to the margins, fated to scavenge what it can from the accumulated waste of data processing on an industrial scale.

It is not beyond our grasp, however, to imagine an alternative world, in which the machines have been replaced with people. These people might still speak of 'data', but they would intend the term to be taken literally, as that which is *given* to them, so that they might live and know. They accept, with good grace, what the world offers to them, rather than attempting to extract – whether by force or subterfuge – what it does not. They are nourished by this offering, just as they are by the food they eat, and, as with food, they go on to digest it. But for them digestion is, above all, a process of life and growth. In producing knowledge, then, they are also producing their own selves as people who know. They are of course aware that any such process entails a degree of friction: not everything can be incorporated into growth and some things pass through undigested. There is surely no craft that does not, in the fashioning of its materials, generate copious quantities of waste, whether in the form of dust, shavings, chips or off-cuts. It is no different with the crafts of the intellect. But in this alternative world, waste is not knowledge. It only becomes knowledge when it is re-entered into a process of life.

No living being, however, can persist indefinitely, nor can it carry on its life in isolation. The continuity of life – and hence of knowledge too – requires of every being that it should play its part in bringing other lives into existence and sustaining them for however long it takes for the latter, in turn, to engender further life. It follows that all living, and all knowing, is intrinsically social, whether it be of trees in a wood, beasts in a herd or human beings in a community. Social life is one long correspondence. More precisely, it is a tangled mesh of correspondences, all going on concurrently, which weave into and around one another. They run, spinning here and there into topics like eddies in a stream. And they have three distinguishing properties. First, every correspondence is a *process*: it carries on. Secondly, correspondence is *open-ended*: it aims for no fixed destination or final conclusion, for everything that might be said or done invites a follow-on. Thirdly, correspondences are *dialogical*. They are not solitary but go on between and among participants. It is from these dialogical engagements that knowledge continually arises. To correspond is to be ever-present at the cusp where thinking is on the point of settling into the shapes of thought. It is to catch ideas on the fly, in the ferment of their incipience, lest they be washed away with the current and forever lost.

The rigour of amateurs

In the correspondences that make up this book, I have revelled in the freedom to throw off the shackles of academic convention, and to write unashamedly as an amateur. All true scholars, I believe, are amateurs. Literally, the amateur is one who studies a topic not – like the professional – in order to stage a career, but for the love of it, motivated by a sense of care, personal involvement and responsibility. Amateurs are correspondents. And in study they find a way of life that harmonizes with their whole way of living in the world. Admittedly, this appeal to amateurism is not without its pitfalls, especially in a political climate in which professional expertise is routinely dismissed as the posturing of a technocratic elite more interested in shoring up their own status and privilege than in listening to the common sense of ordinary, unlettered folk. Something must be added to our definition of what it means to be an amateur, lest we risk a descent into crude populism.

On reflection, the two words I think we need are *rigour* and *precision*. Amateur study, to be worthy of the name, must be rigorous and precise. Both terms, however, call for some unpacking. Thinking about the idea of rigour initially put me in mind of my own lifelong attempts, as an amateur musician, to master the cello. While they have involved years of practice, struggle, frustration and even pain, they have nevertheless brought a great sense of personal fulfilment. Rigour has its rewards. Recently, however, I had the good fortune to read an article by the artist and visual anthropologist Amanda Ravetz, and it forced me to think again.[4] Ravetz is concerned with what it means to say of art that it is a process of research, in a context in which research of all kinds is coming under increasingly prescriptive regimes of assessment. Currently, the gold standard for research rests on three criteria: originality, rigour and significance. It is not unreasonable, Ravetz thinks, to judge artistic research by its significance and originality. Rigour, however, risks killing it off. But is this the same rigour, I wondered, that I bring to my cello practice?

One can question the etymology of the word. Ravetz traces it to the Middle English variants of *rig*, covering everything from the strip of the medieval ploughman to the spine of an animal and the roof-ridge of a house. My dictionary, however, finds the root of the word in the Latin *rigere*, 'to be stiff', with the further connotations of rectitude, rigidity, numbness and morbidity. Whichever derivation you prefer – and perhaps they are connected – hardness and severity seem to be at the heart of it. Rigour is bereft of feeling, yields nothing to experience, and induces instant paralysis in anything living or moving with which it might come into contact. Is this the way of the so-called 'hard sciences'? Then it is one to which the amateur scholar must be resolutely opposed. For having chosen to align his or her entire life and being with the subject of study, the amateur seeks a softer and more sympathetic approach, one that both answers to the call of the subject and is in turn answerable to it. The response is tinged with responsibility, curiosity with care. There is what Ravetz calls a 'correspondence with felt vitality'. And for her, this correspondence is anything but rigorous. This doesn't mean that it is thoughtless, bland or insensitive to difference. The conventional opposition between expertise and common sense tends to imagine the former as consisting of peaks of knowledge, rising from an otherwise homogeneous and featureless plateau. The landscape of correspondence, however, is infinitely variegated. To correspond with things is to follow these variations. 'The thinking that joins with things,' as Ravetz puts it, is 'heterogeneous, emergent, situated and cloudy.'⁵ It is continuously in touch with feeling, with lived experience. What does it mean, then, to study along these lines?

We are dealing, here, with a contrast between two kinds of thinking. There's a thinking that joins things *up*, and a thinking that joins *with* things. In one case the things have already precipitated out, as data, from the processes of their formation; the task, then, is retrospectively to reconnect them. In the other, the things are ever-emergent, and the task is to enter into the forward movement of their ongoing generation. Consider, for example, the straight line, famously defined by Euclid as the shortest connection between points. Determine the points, and you have already specified the line. This line has no breadth; it is abstract and insensible. It is not like the taut strings of my cello, which have a certain weight and thickness, and which, moreover, bend and vibrate when bowed or plucked. It is not like the straight furrow of the ploughman that is cut as he goes along, and calls for his constant and vigilant attention so as to maintain its equidistance from, and alignment with, the adjacent rig. It is not like the rigging of the ship, which in its alternating tension and relaxation allows for the precise adjustment of the sails in response to prevailing winds. Nor is it like the perfectly straight lines that the artist Jaime Refoyo taught me to draw freehand, but only after having first instructed me in how to find a certain balance of forces and muscular tensions within my own body, calling also for a heightened perceptual awareness of my immediate surroundings. If there is rigour in these lines, it is neither immobile nor insentient. It lies, rather, in the precision of close attunement: in the tension of the cello string, yielding a determinate pitch on vibration; in the ploughman's attention to the field; in the mariner's attention to the wind; in my attention to my body and its environs.

It would seem that there are two varieties of rigour, virtually the opposite of each other: one that demands accuracy in the recording, measurement and integration of an unyielding world of objective facts; the other that calls for practised care and attentiveness in an ongoing relation between conscious awareness and lively materials. In the latter, and not the former, lies the rigour of correspondence. And this is where precision comes in. For it should not be confused with accuracy. Dancers, for example, are precise rather than accurate in the observations that allow them to attune their movements to one another. Here, precision rests on the capacity to flex in response to others' movements. The same goes for any kind of craft, where the skill of the practitioner lies in an ability to attune the movements of the sensing body to tools and materials in a way that calls forth relations of line, surface, scale and proportion. The dancer and the artisan are amateurs. They are amateurs because their dance, their craft, proceeds along a way of life. Their practice is careful, attentive, rigorous, but its rigour is of the second kind. Let's call it amateur rigour, a rigour that is flexible and in love with life, by contrast to the professional rigour that induces rigidity and paralysis.

The way of art

Corresponding with as much rigour and precision as I can command, I have tried in these essays to stay close to the grain of things. I want to show that the practice of thinking we often call 'theory' doesn't mean having to lift off into a stratospheric realm of hyper-abstraction, or to mingle in our imagination with concepts that have drifted so far from the ground of experience, to which they owe their origin, as to have lost all touch with it. Quite to the contrary, theoretical work can be as much grounded in the materials and forces of the inhabited world as the conduct of any other craft. To practise theory as a mode of habitation is to mix and mingle, in one's thinking, with the textures of the world. This means, if you will, not taking literal truths metaphorically, but *taking metaphorical truths literally*. The theorist can be a poet. For example, inspired by the poetry of Seamus Heaney, I might compare my digging for words to the crofter's digging for peat, and my pen to a spade.[6] I would be urged on by an intuition that a deeper truth lurks within the comparison, and in my theorizing, that's the truth I'm trying to find. And I know that I'll have a greater chance of finding it by going to ground than by lifting off. I should pick up a spade and dig! I should think, as I do so, of what the spade is telling me about the earth, or rather of what the earth is telling me through the spade. And I can then bring the lessons I have learned to my thinking on the page.

Taking metaphorical truths literally, however, is not just the way of poetry; it is also – and perhaps above all – the way of art. The work of the artist is to embody such truths, to make them viscerally present to us, so that we can experience them in their immediacy. The majority of essays gathered here were originally written in response to artistic provocations. Some were commissioned by the artists themselves, or by the curators of their works; others were composed on my own initiative. It is not my purpose to make any judgement, aesthetic or otherwise, of the art itself. I offer no expert interpretation or analysis. I write as an amateur respondent, not a professional critic. But working in the medium of words, I have set out to insert my own voice into the correspondence. And to be honest, I have very much enjoyed doing so. It has been a relief to drop my academic persona and write with my own voice, hand and heart. Above all, I have relished the freedom both to embrace fresh ideas and to be shaken up and disturbed by them.

The twenty-seven essays making up the book are grouped into six parts. We begin in the woods, conversing with trees, then trace an arc from sea to land to sky and back down to earth. We go to ground, mix with the elements, follow lines and threads from the gatherings of nature to the pages of the book, and conclude with a plea to restore words to the hand. Although the journey itself, proceeding in gradual steps from world to words, unfolds without interruption, it is assembled out of singular elements each of which – taken on its own – has its own character and integrity. Rather like a bird's nest, it is constructed from assorted fragments that were never designed to fit together. The contingent coherence of the nest, and the latitude it affords to its constituents, gives it a resilience thanks to which it hangs together even under the most adverse of weather conditions. Irregularity holds it fast. It is the same with this book, affording the reader the latitude to dip in at any point, to read the essays in any order, and perhaps to circle back to look at some again. Like walking in the woods, you can take any number of alternative routes. Think of the book's pages, then, as the ground on which you walk, and of its lines as paths. Happy wandering!

TALES FROM THE WOODS

Introduction

Can there be any better example of conviviality, of living and growing together, than the trees of a wood? They are so much more sociable than people. Humans come and go, obsessed by passing troubles. But trees stand their ground. They tell tales, they communicate among themselves; older trees watch over young saplings, which sprout amidst the roots of their forebears. We humans are but diminutive eavesdroppers on their long, majestic conversations. Enter the woods, then, as into a library or a cathedral, with a certain reverence. Sociology begins here, in your studies with the trees. Ahead of you, like rows of books on the shelves, or the columns of the nave, are the serried ranks of trunks. Each trunk – each *codex*, as the ancients called both trunk and book – holds its story, not between its covers, as with the book, but up aloft, as with the fan-vaulting of the cathedral roof or the branching tracery of its windows. You'll need to strain your neck to read it.

Peer closely into the canopy, listen intently, feel the textures of bark and moss as if they were under your skin or fingernails. No doubt you feel more alive in the presence of trees. Yet to us, they seem to speak in riddles. Even as we strain to decipher their meanings, we sense no progress towards clarity. In the woods, everything is so complicated! It is, quite literally, folded together – from the Latin *com*, 'together' plus *plicare*, 'to fold'. Of the trees that gather there, we cannot say where one ends and another begins. They don't adjoin or abut like fragments of a mosaic, or square up back to back, each sunk into itself. Rather, they fold over and into each other as they go along. Observe the ground, riddled with roots that threaten to trip you up, the ridged and furrowed tree bark, the ruffled wind-swept mass of foliage. Every line of the gathering is a fold in the fabric of a crumpled world.

But crumples are alien to our desire for order. We prefer a world that answers to the call of reason. Whenever we build or make, we endeavour to straighten things out, to simplify. We like external surfaces to be smooth and flat, and angles sharp. Perhaps we envy the trees their complicated conviviality. We cannot countenance the thought that they might enjoy a way of living together, in peace and tranquillity, that to us remains unfathomable. 'It's them or us,' we say; 'there's no more room for both.' Needing land for cattle and plantations, timber for ships and cellulose for the paper industry, humans through history have hacked the woods, or put them to the torch. Even as I write these lines, regions of the planet are in flames, their inhabitants fleeing for their lives. After the conflagration, the woods will once more rise from the ashes. But human society? Maybe; but maybe not.

Somewhere in Northern Karelia . . .

On New Year's Day, 2016, I – along with some thirty others – received an invitation from the writer and broadcaster Tim Dee to compose an essay on the topic of a place that personally speaks to me. Tired of the numbing combination of facts and spirituality that permeates so much contemporary environmental writing, Dee wanted to show how precious ordinary places are to us, and why it is so important that we continue to care for them. A place, we were told, could be anything or anywhere. It might be a hollow tree or the corner of a street, a childhood bedroom or a sewage farm. It could be in the paved world of the city, with its streets and buildings, or in the vegetated world of the countryside, with its fields and forests. All that mattered was that it should be close to our hearts. The essays would eventually be assembled into a book. Entitled Ground Work, *the book was published in 2018.*[1]

I decided to focus my essay on a place especially dear to me. Indeed, many of the ideas gathered in this book first took root there. This essay, therefore, seemed like a fitting place from which to embark on the correspondences to come.

Somewhere in the woods of Northern Karelia lies a huge boulder. Once it rode a glacier as a wandering erratic, having been torn from granite bedrock by the force of moving ice. Then, when the ice melted, it was unceremoniously dumped on a steep incline. It has remained there ever since, ever about to roll down the hill but never quite doing so, as soil, moss, lichen, shrubs and trees have grown up all around it. The boulder has become its own environment, providing shade and shelter for plants on the lower side, and surfaces for other plants to grow upon; there is even a pine sapling rooted in a fissure near the top. Deep in the forest, you have to pick your way over rocks and wade through a carpet of vegetation to find it. Standing some four metres tall, with an equivalent girth in all directions, what meets your eyes is about two hundred tons of rock, not settled flat on the ground but falling down the slope with a velocity of zero. Only a precarious balance of forces holds it there. But at some time in the past – possibly thousands of years ago – it was rent asunder. Water must have penetrated a crack, expanded when it froze, and, with immense force, split the boulder from top to bottom, breaking off a massive slab that at the same time shifted some seventy centimetres to the side. The wedge-shaped crack remains open at the top, and a small block of stone has fallen into it, where it remains jammed, about a third of the way down. Another shard of rock has slid from the cracked face and rests on the block exactly as it fell, supported on its sharp edge (Figure 1). All this must have happened in a split second, and in the stillness of the forest I try to imagine the explosive sound it would

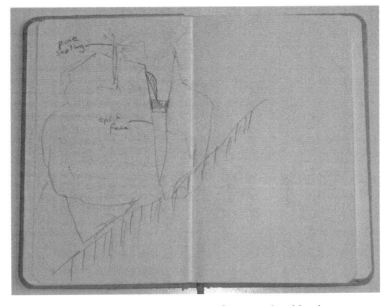

Figure 1 The boulder: a page from my sketchbook.
(Photo by the author.)

have made, and how it would have echoed through the landscape. Looking at the precariously balanced assembly, of shard on block, of block in crack, of crack in boulder, of boulder on incline, I have the feeling that I inhabit a silence on the inside of the explosion. It is as if nature, in this boulder, were forever holding its breath. One day it will give way, and the boulder will tumble down. We cannot know when that will be. Best not to be beneath it when it does!

Somewhere in these woods is a special tree. It is not large, nor has it grown to any great height. At its foot, its roots are tightly wrapped around an outcrop of glacier-smoothed rock, from which a thick, gnarled trunk coils out like a snake, eventually inclining towards the vertical as it thins into more recent growth, dissolving into a spray of needle-covered branches and twigs. The tree is a pine, and thanks to its location on the shore of a great lake, it has known extremes of wind and cold from which its larger inland cousins are somewhat protected. Its twisted trunk bears witness to early years of struggle against the elements, when once it was but a young and slender sapling. Deep inside, that sapling is still there, buried beneath decades of further growth and accretion. Now hardened and gnarled with age, my tree can hold out against anything that nature might throw at it. What for me is so special about this tree, however, is the way it seems to establish a sort of conversation between rock and air. At base the wood has all but turned to stone. The roots, following the contours of the outcrop and penetrating its crevasses, hold the rock in an iron grip. But up above, delicate needles vibrate to the merest puff of wind and play host to tiny geometrid caterpillars that measure out the twigs in their peculiar looping gait. How is it possible for such ageless solidity and ephemeral volatility to be brought into unison? This is the miracle of my tree. Through it, the rock opens up to meet the sky, while the annual passage of seasons nestles within what seems like an eternity. To spend time with this tree, as I have done, is at once to be of the moment and to sink back into a reverie of agelessness.

Here in these woods, forest ants are at work, building their nest. From a distance the nest reveals itself as a perfectly formed mound, circular in plan and bell-shaped in elevation. Observe it closely, however, and it turns out to be seething with movement as legions of ants jostle with one another and with the materials they have brought back – mostly grains of sand and pine-needles. From the centre, ant-roads fan out in all directions. You have to peer at the ground to see them. Often they are more like tunnels, boring their way through the dense carpet of mosses and lichens that covers the earth. If you were the size of an ant, the challenges of the passage would be formidable, as what to us are mere pebbles would present precipitous climbs and vertical drops, while tree-roots would be mountain ranges. Yet nothing seems to deter the traffic as thousands upon thousands of ants march out and back, the outward goers often colliding with returnees laden with materials of some sort to add to the heap. Wandering alone in the forest, it is odd to think that beneath one's feet are miniature insect imperia, populated by millions, of unimaginable strangeness and complexity.

In the woods the wind is blowing. You can hear it coming from a long way off, especially through the aspen trees. Each tree hands it on to the next until, for a moment, their leaves are all singing to the same tune. Every leaf is aquiver, even though the trunks sway only a little. Then all is quiet again. The gust has moved on. On the waters of the lake the surface is disturbed into ripples which focus the reflected light into little suns that flash first double and then single. As the ripples reach the lakeshore, the reeds bend over, rustling in unison, until they in turn fall silent. Do trees create the gust of wind by waving their leaf-draped limbs? Does water create wind by rippling? Do reeds create wind by rustling? Of course not! Yet, surely, the clarinettist needs a reed to turn his breath into music. So if, by wind, we mean its music to our ears, or its sun-dance to our eyes, then yes – leaves, ripples and reeds do make the wind. For when I say I hear the wind, or see it in the surface of the lake, the sounds I hear are made by leaves just as much as is the light I see made by ripples.

Once I was flying a kite out on the field, where the grass had recently been cut. As I played on the string, it seemed to me that my kite, like the leaves of the trees, was also an instrument for turning aerial gusts into music in motion. However, the string, often entangled on previous flights, had been repaired at many points by cutting and retying. An unusually strong gust overwhelmed one of the knots and my kite broke loose. Off it went, sailing over the tree-tops, buoyed up by the wind. I imagine the kite having relished its new-found freedom. 'Watch me,' it would have crowed. 'I am a creature of the sky. Field and forest, they are all the same to me!' But its dreams were to come to an ignominious end as it drifted down to earth. Most likely it was snagged on an angling tree-branch as it fell. I never found it again. But I am sure it is there, somewhere in the woods, draped forlornly from the branch, utterly lost.

I too, in straying from field to forest, have risked becoming lost. I know an old path that runs through the woods, though I am not sure where it begins, and it ends in the middle of nowhere. Long ago, however, it was made by the passage of many feet as people, year in year out, would go with rakes, scythes and pitchforks from the farms around the lake to cut the hay in far-flung meadows. The hay would be stored in field-barns and brought in by horse and sledge over the winter to feed the cattle in their stalls. But that was in the past. First the horses went, as every farm acquired a tractor. Then the outfields were abandoned, as forestry became more profitable than dairy production. Then the cows were sold off, and finally the people left. Few farms remain inhabited year-round. And so the path fell out of use and is gradually fading. In places it has completely disappeared. Trees have fallen across it or are even growing in its midst. I can tell the path is there only by following a line of subtle variation in the leaf-mould on the ground, a gap in lichen cover, a thinning of soil on rock. So long as I am on it, I can discern the path by running my eye along the line. But I know that if I move to one side or the other, the line will disappear. Indeed this has happened to me on more than one occasion: having deviated from the path in one direction – my attention drawn by an anthill or by luscious bilberries to pick – I have crossed right over it on the return without even noticing, and strayed too far in the opposite direction. How, then, should we think of this path, which is visible only as you go along it? It is a line made by walking; an inscription of human activity on the land. Yet while one can distinguish the path from the ground in which it is inscribed – albeit only faintly and with an eye already tuned to its presence – it is not possible to distinguish the ground from the path. For the ground is not a base upon which every feature is mounted like scenery on a stage set. It is rather a surface that is multiply folded and crumpled. The path is like a fold in the ground.

Somewhere in Northern Karelia there are still cows. But here there are none. The fields fell silent many years ago. Once we would row across the lake with a churn to fetch milk, warm and fresh, from the dairy. But these days, it doesn't pay to look after a few head of cattle, and anyway, who will do the milking when the old folk retire? No girl wants to follow her mother into the cowshed; no boy aspires to what has always been seen as women's work. Nowadays cattle are concentrated in big production facilities, whose managers rent the fields once used for grazing to provide a year-round supply of fodder. Sometimes I imagine that the cows are still there, wandering the fields like ghosts. I think I see them staring asquint with their doleful moon-eyes, and hear them lowing, chewing the cud, crashing through undergrowth. Then silence falls again, pierced only by the wistful cry of the curlew. Where the cows once lingered, strange white oval forms can be seen scattered here and there over the meadows, or lined up on their trackside perimeters. People call them 'dinosaur eggs'. Really, they are gigantic rolls of machine-cut hay. The machine rolls the hay as it cuts, and as each roll is completed, it is automatically wrapped in white plastic sheeting and laid – like a great egg – on the ground. Later, the 'eggs' will be collected and taken far away, to the place where all the cows are now.

Amidst fields bordered by woods and lake stands an old timber-built cottage. As a family, we have often spent our summers here. The cottage has a living room, two small bedrooms, a porch and a little veranda. Outside, a set of wooden steps leads up to the front door. Every morning I sit on the steps and think. I think about all the life that has passed there, from when our children were taking their first steps to now when they have families of their own. I listen to the birds, watch the bees as they pollinate the flowers, follow the sun as it passes between the trees, and drink a mug of tea. And I think about what I am going to write that day. If the weather is fine, I write outside at a small wooden table, seated on a bench hewn from a log, and look across the yard to the trees on the other side. The table is covered by a plastic-coated cloth, which is bare apart from a tin on which I mount a spiral of insect repellent. I light one end and it burns very slowly, giving off a sweetly aromatic smoke that is alleged to drive away the mosquitoes that might otherwise invade my writing space. It is hardly needed as there are fewer mosquitoes these days – an effect of climate change perhaps – and I'm not even sure that they take much notice of the smoke. But I burn it anyway, as I quite like the smell. It is a sign that I am thinking. As the spiral of repellent is slowly consumed, it seems to me that my thoughts curl up, like the smoke, and waft into air.

For the rest of the year, when I am not here, I dream about my bench and table and about the steps to the cottage. Nowhere is there a more tranquil place to be. Nowhere is more conducive to intense reflection, for my mind can withstand the stress of churning thought only when it is otherwise at peace. And nowhere are the multiple rhythms of the world, from the glacial to the atmospheric, more perfectly nested. The cracked boulder, the twisted tree, the empire of the ants, the sighing wind and the suns that reflect from ripples on the lake, the memory of a lost kite, the fading path and absent cows, the dinosaur eggs, the steps on which I sit and the table at which I write these lines: these are among the many stories woven into the fabric of my favourite place. I won't tell you exactly where it is, as this would give away my secret. But it is somewhere in Northern Karelia.

Pitch black and firelight

*David Nash is a sculptor who works on a large scale, with the wood of whole trees. Lately, he has taken to setting the wood ablaze. In one work (*Black Trunk, *2010*) *he enveloped the trunk of a redwood tree in planks and set it on fire. For a while the rising conflagration lit the sky, but when it was over the trunk remained standing. It is standing still, gaunt and black as charcoal. But its blackness does not betoken death and destruction. Quite to the contrary, it is as though the charred trunk, like a black hole, had sucked into itself all the energy of the blaze. It endures as a concentration of strength, power and vitality, ready to burst into life at any time.*

Nash's work got me thinking about how wood, the mother of all materials, is related to light, the giver of all life. I recalled that besides solid charcoal, burned pine also releases a liquid residue which coagulates as pitch. What kind of substance is this, blacker even than charcoal? And how does its blackness compare with that of a pitch-dark night?[1]

In the beginning was a pine tree. There it stood, its roots bedded in the hard ground, its upright trunk firm but thinning towards the tip, its branches and twigs swaying in the wind, all adorned with fine green needles quivering in the sunshine.

Then the navy started to build great ships, for which it needed quantities of timber. Our tree, along with countless neighbours, was felled. Brought to the sawmill, the trunk was cut into square-faced planks and beams. But for a while at least, the stump and roots remained in the ground. The ships, however, needed more than wood. They needed tar to coat the sails, ropes and rigging, in order to waterproof them and to protect them from rot. And they needed pitch to caulk the timbers, to ensure that no water could seep into the joints. For this purpose, the remaining stump was rooted up. Hacked into pieces, it was placed in a furnace and fired. The wood turned to charcoal, but at the base of the furnace, a dark brown sticky liquid ran out along a pipe, at the end of which it was collected in a bucket. This was tar. To make pitch, the tar was boiled in a cauldron, driving off the aqueous content as steam. The result was a thick, highly viscous fluid that would dry into a hard lump. But however solid it appears when dried, pitch remains fluid. It just flows very, very slowly. In colour, it is absolutely black.

In the story of the tree, what began with the white light of the sun caught in its canopy of needles ended with the blackness of pitch, drawn off from its roots and stump in their consumption by fire. Here, what happened to wood, as it was reduced to pitch, was also what happened to light, as it was extinguished. The story tells of wood and light, and its theme rests in their affinity.

To pursue this theme, let us return to the sawmill, where the trunk has been turned into beams. These days we also speak of beams of light. When the rays of the sun, low in the sky, glance through broken cloud, we say we see sunbeams. In Latin they were known as *radii solis*, 'spokes of the sun'. But why should these spokes have entered the vernacular of English as 'beams'? What do sunbeams and beams of wood have in common that would have led to the same word being applied to both? Could it have been their evident straightness? The wooden beam is a straight length of timber of thick, rectangular section, destined to carry a heavy structural load. The light beam is a ray, or a bundle of parallel rays, as of the sun or emitted from a candle. What they share, it seems, is clear-cut rectilinearity.

Yet within every beam of wood, in its grain, knots and rings, lurk the vestiges of the living tree from which it was once cut. And so, likewise, the word itself harbours traces of its past usage. In Old English, 'beam' simply meant any tree: not yet cut but alive and growing in the ground. Though otherwise obsolete, this usage survives in the names of common tree species such as hornbeam, whitebeam and quickbeam (also known as rowan or mountain ash). In this original sense the tree is a beam not because it is especially straight but because it rises like a column from the earth. Beaming is upward growth.

Remarkably, this is also the sense in which we first hear of beams of light. This was the light of a fire. The beam was the flame, shooting upwards into the air as the tree-trunk rises from the ground, not perfectly straight but twisting and turning in response to atmospheric conditions. It was the equivalent of the biblical *columna lucis*, the 'pillar of light' by which, in the Book of Exodus, the Israelites were guided on their way at night. The Venerable Bede, writing in the eighth century, used the word 'beam' in precisely this way to describe the column of light or fire ascending from the body of a saint. For Bede, as the tree-trunk grows from the earth, so light rises from the saintly body.[2]

Thus conceived, however, the beam of light is quite different from the ray. The ray is a line of emission, radiating from a source of energy as a spoke from the centre of a wheel. When we draw the sun, or a candle flame, it is conventional to depict rays of light as straight lines fanning out in all directions. This convention, too, gives us the familiar pointed form of the star. The beam, by contrast, is neither perfectly straight nor does it point in any direction. Rather than issuing from a source, the beam-line describes the growth or movement – literally the beaming – of the source itself. It is a line of combustion. It can flicker like a candle flame, zigzag like forked lightning, streak like a shooting star. Even sunbeams are depicted, in early medieval sources, as the twirling flames of a great fireball (Figure 2).

Ray and beam, I suggest, afford alternative ways of thinking about light: what it is, how it moves, and how it is apprehended. On the one hand, as ray, it is an energetic impulse that connects a point source to the eye of a recipient, across what could be an immense void of space; on the other hand, as beam, it is an affectation of visual awareness – an explosion that ignites as much in the eye of the beholder as in the world beholden. For in the moment of its apprehension, eye and cosmos become one. If a tree could see, its leaves would be miniature eyes, and the glimmer in each – as it strains to find its place in the sun – would be drawn down twigs and branches into a great beam.

Figure 2 The sun and the moon. Detail from a painting from the wooden ceiling of the stave-church of Ål, in central Norway, dating from the thirteenth century. (Courtesy of the Museum of Cultural History, University of Oslo.)

Where we onlookers would see a solid trunk, the tree would open in its vision to a world on fire. It would be a creature of the light.

But it could be a creature of the dark as well. If there are two ways of thinking about light, then darkness, too, can also mean different things. It can mean the darkness of shade, such as when the rays of the sun, striking a solid and opaque body, cast a shadow on the ground, or when, at night, the earth shadows itself. Or it can mean the darkness that comes from putting out the fire. This is not to block the light but to extinguish it. The 'shadow' of the beam, if we can call it that, is the material residue that falls from the conflagration. The same tree which had once basked in the sun's rays and cast a shadow on the ground *becomes light* in the flames of the fire – as beam rather than rays – and leaves its shadow in the material stuff of ash, charcoal and finally pitch. As ancient and medieval thinkers believed, pitch is born of the element of fire.[3]

Of the blackest of black nights, we say it is pitch-dark. But pitch darkness is one thing, the darkness of pitch another. One is defined negatively, by the absence of radiant light, the other positively, by the presence of material substance. Radiant light – the light of the sun – is said to be white. It is what we get by mixing every shade of the visible spectrum, for example by spinning a top decorated with a colour wheel. When the top is at rest we can distinguish the shades; when it spins they merge into white. These shades, corresponding to wavelengths, give us the colours of the rainbow. All the colour is in the light. No light; no colour. Black, then, is as void of colour as it is of light. The manufacture of pitch, however, tells a different tale.

Let's return, at last, to the tree from which we began. Having cut the trunk for timber, to be sent to the mill, the roots and stump are set alight. What runs out from the light of the fire? Brown tar. What do we get when the tar is boiled to eliminate its water content? Black pitch. As Johann Wolfgang von Goethe famously argued, in his *Theory of Colours* of 1810, black is not the absence of colour but colour at its most concentrated.[4] As pitch is the extract of tar, black is the extract of light: the essence that remains after the light is extinguished. Conversely, to set materials alight is to dilute their colour. So long as the fire burns – like the redwood of Nash's *Black Trunk* – the flames and glowing embers give off shades of yellow and red. But once the fire is extinguished, all shades recede into black. The blackness of pitch, then, is an index not of nothingness but of infinite density, from which colours explode in the ignition of our visual awareness. All colour pours from pitch; and all colour eventually falls back into it.

In the shadow of tree being

Imagine an inside-out world, where breath solidifies but the lungs are vaporized; where the shadow is a body and the body its shadow; where entire landscapes are reflected in the balls of unseeing eyes or gathered under their lids; where trees grow from tips to roots and from the outside in; where these same trees look at us, speak to us, grasp us by the hand and even send us letters; where the forest has us at its fingertips or under its fingernails; where respiration is the rustling of leaves and the nervous system a thornbush.

This is the world of the sculptor Giuseppe Penone, one of the founding figures of the movement in Italian art known as Arte povera, *which took off in the late 1960s and early 1970s. I do not, in this essay, write about Penone, or about his art. I make no reference to it at all. The path I follow is my own, and yet, like his, it winds through woods, through nature and through life. As we go along our respective paths, his and mine, they touch at many points. I am interested in these tangents. What follows, then, is an exercise in thinking along the same lines, but in words rather than works. It is a way of thinking that proceeds by analogy and inversion, in which everything and everybody – ourselves included – has its double and is made whole by its restoration.*

But it is also a way to which words are, in many respects, ill suited. This essay – originally commissioned by the Gagosian, New York, for a retrospective review of Penone's forty-year artistic career, and reproduced here in an abridged version – has not been easy to write.[1] Indeed, my efforts seem threadbare by comparison to the works with which they correspond. The scholar's verbal impulse to explicate continually threatens to unravel the dense weave of experience. But that, of course, is precisely the point. It is why there can be no substitute for art. Do not, then, expect an explanation or interpretation, or that I should put the art in its social, cultural or historical context. I will have none of that. My purpose is to think with it.

Body

There are two halves to every body. One half is made of flesh, and wrapped in skin. That's the half we can see. The other half, normally invisible to us, is made of air. Even as we breathe, these two halves run in and out of one another. This is possible because the skin is no simple covering, separating the bodily substance on the inside from the medium of air without, but a surface of extraordinary topological complexity, infolding at the various orifices that afford metabolic exchange with the environment to give way internally to a veritable labyrinth of branching ducts, tubules and capillaries. Though the aerial half of the body is always with us – though we could not live without it – we are inclined to ignore it, believing ourselves to be creatures entirely of the flesh.

In the woods, too, we tend to see only one half of every tree. We forget the wind. The wind is the tree's double: there can no more be a living tree without wind than a living body without breath. We cannot see the breath of trees, but we can hear it in the rustling of leaves as the wind wraps around them. The surface of the leaf, with its veins and corpuscles, is not an outer covering but an interior fold, wherein the visible part of the tree is brought into contact with its invisible double.

Every surface is a fold in the fabric of the world. As with the leaf, so too the skin is a fold in the body, where flesh makes contact with air. Imagine a body turned inside out, such that its breath is of the earth, and its flesh of the air. What would it look like? Let us fashion such a body from the earthy material of clay. The mouth, moulded to the contours of the oral cavity, would appear as an oddly shaped lump, and every exhalation would be formed as an immense urn, broadening out towards a rounded base where it pours forth into the surrounding atmosphere, and ruffled along the sides by the turbulence set up in its wake (Figure 3). Of the flesh, now aerial, we would see nothing,

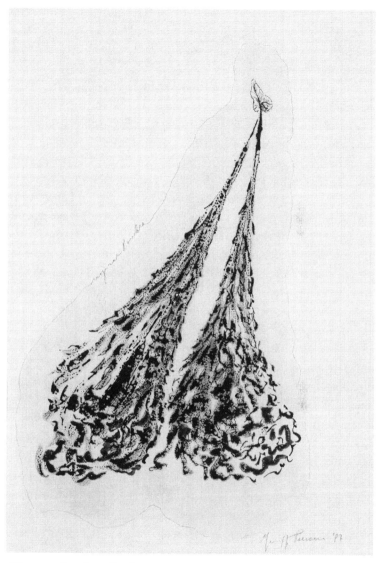

Figure 3 *Respirare l'ombra* [Breathe the shadow], drawing by Giuseppe Penone, 1987. (Courtesy of the Gagosian Gallery.)

but in its midst would be formed a tree-like structure, its trunk the windpipe, its branches and twigs the bronchial and bronchiolar tubes, its leaves the alveoli, seemingly growing downwards from its germinal root in the mouth.

The figure we have created turns out to be a tree being! What is substantial in the body of the human being is aerial in the tree being, and vice versa. Thus, the tree allows us to see what is invisible in ourselves: the dendritic structure reveals the lungs, the root-ball the mouth, the shape of the canopy the breath. Give the tree a mouth, and it will sing like a flute. But the flute and the tree – both woodwind instruments – work in inverse ways. With the flute, wind passes through wood to produce melodious sound; with the tree, wood passes through wind to produce a line of growth. Every branch or twig is the solid equivalent of a melodic line. Trees even breathe in reverse: what we breathe in, the trees breathe out. Body and tree are like hand and glove.

Shadow

Everything there is, in this world, is both bound to the earth and under the sun, subject to the former's gravitation and the latter's illumination. Tree being is a creature of sky and earth, wind and clay, light and sound. A solid body, placed on the earth and under the blazing sun, casts a shadow. The body has substance, but the shadow has none, apart from that of the ground on which it is projected. Moreover, it comes and goes. Whenever the sun vanishes behind a cloud, the shadow also disappears, not because the cloud blocks out the sun's rays but because they are dispersed in all directions by atmospheric vapour. What is this ephemeral, quixotic shadow telling us? It tells us that existence is a temporal thing, and that our fragile lives are ever-suspended betwixt heaven and earth, sensitive at every moment to the time of day, the passage of seasons and the vagaries of weather. Shadows reveal to us that we are temperamental creatures, formed in the elemental mixture of light and air.

A shadow is a different thing, however, if, comparing light to the living tree, we think of it as beam rather than ray. With rays, shadows are projections, casting outlines on the ground of the objects on which they fall, extended and distorted depending on the angle of incidence and the lie of the land. But the shadow of the beam is its negative, an impression, more akin to a footprint or handprint, or the markings on a photographic plate. If the light beam rises like a column from the earth, then the shadow falls as a deposit in its wake. Ash is the shadow of a woodfire, a collapsed mound of wax the shadow of a candle, pitch the shadow of pine. Grease is the shadow of fingers and sweaty palms on the tools we use, on the handles with which we open doors, and on the turned pages of well-thumbed books. Ash, wax, pitch and grease: these shadows have substance. They are not projections of rigid form but the residues of material flows, admixtures and mutations.

Everything leaves a shadow-trace of some sort. But the body of the thing can no more be detached from its shadow than it can be removed from the world in which it exists. We know that a person has been by their footprints in the soil. Anatomically, perhaps, as a structure of flesh and bone, the foot is part of the body, but in our experience of walking, it is only a foot in its contact with the earth; and the earth we walk exists for us only because of the way we feel it with our feet. Thus we cannot say that the foot belongs to the human and the print to the earth. Rather, both foot and print are complementary aspects of the one earth-human. Is it any different with trees? Every autumn, deciduous trees drop their leaves, which form a thick carpet on the ground around and about. The carpet, we could say, is the material shadow of the beaming tree. Yet even when parted from the branches and twigs on which they once grew, leaves never lose their vital connection with tree being. Like the prints of many feet, the leaves of countless trees mingle to form a palimpsest of shadow on the surface of the earth.

Touch

Go into the woods and find a slender tree, of such girth that you can readily grasp the trunk between the thumb and fingers of your hand. Grasp it tight, so tight that you can feel the serrations of the bark as they bite into your flesh. There can be no doubt that you are touching the tree. But is the tree touching you? What is happening in that invisible place of surface-to-surface contact, where skin meets bark? How, moreover, can you be so confident that you are touching the tree, when only a small area lies under your hand?

Ostensibly, tree and human are beings of very different kinds. The human has a nervous system which allows it not only to register any tactile sensation but also to position it. A sensation triggered at any point in the system affects the system as a whole. That is why, when you grasp the tree, you are sure that you feel it. It is a feeling, moreover, that radiates from the area of contact throughout the body. You feel the tree with your entire being. Were you to substitute, for your hand, a replica cast in metal, there would be no such touch, and no feeling. But what about the tree? Would it notice the difference between a human hand and its metallic replica? Would it notice anything at all?

The tree has no nervous system, and cannot therefore feel as a human can. But it is nevertheless a living thing. It respires; it draws nutrients from the earth in its sap; its surfaces – of roots, bark and leaves – are porous and afford continuous interchange of substance with air above and soil below. For that reason, the tree is affected by the grasp of the iron hand, and it responds in the way its materials, in their flows and transformations, accommodate to the intruding presence. As the tree swells under the impress of the intruder, the hand is gradually sucked in, to the point at which it becomes irremovable. Grown together over many years, tree and hand become one.

Touch is different, then, depending on whether it entails mere physical contact, organic response or nervous stimulation. Human skin is the most sensitive of surfaces, so crowded with nerve-endings that, in magnification, it would make a bed of thorns of every surface with which it comes into contact. Touch a thornbush and it is you, and not the bush, that feels the prick. Tree-bark, though rough, does not do the same to skin. It does, however, deform under pressure, like a moist sponge that wraps around the fingers as they squeeze. But whether through prick or squeeze, the paradox of touch is that while no form of contact can be more intimate, none is also more emphatic in affirming the separation of the sensor and the sensed. It is at the surface that this separation is established. For were the surface to dissolve, toucher and touched would run into one another, like water drops on meeting and merging, so as to become literally indistinguishable.

Time

Archaeologists like to go back in time. In their practices of excavation, they remove layer after layer of material, assigning the artefacts they find embedded in it to their appropriate positions in what they call 'the record'. It is a timeline in which everything has a date. This stone tool, it is from a hundred thousand years ago; this ivory carving from ten thousand years ago; this fragment of pottery from just a thousand years ago. But what does it mean to say of these things that they have a certain antiquity? Does it even make sense to ask how old they are? The stone, after all, was there for aeons before it was quarried and fashioned into a tool, and is still with us now. The ivory once grew as the tusk of a mammoth roaming the steppe-tundra; the clay was formed as a deposit in the earth long before the potter dug it up for his raw material. The dates we assign to artefacts, at the point of fabrication, are but passing moments in the never-ending lives of the materials of which they are made.

Or consider an ordinary item of furniture, like a table. We know the year it was made: when a carpenter set to work with regular beams and planks, sawn and planed from seasoned wood, to fashion the assembly. Yet every beam or plank still bespeaks the tree from which it once was hewn (Figure 4). The tree is older than the table. But then, how old is it? Of course there was a moment when it must have germinated from a parent seed. But at that time, it was not yet wood, not even a sapling, but a soft and delicate green shoot. The tree is not just older than the table; it is older than its wood! Nor is there any reason to stop there. For the seed retains its vital connection with the tree on which it once grew: both parental tree and seedling are part of

Figure 4 *Gli alberi dei travi* [The trees of the beams], drawing by
Giuseppe Penone, 1970. (Courtesy of the Gagosian Gallery.)

the same cycle of life. The tree, in short, has no point of origin, since
it is originating all the time. And continual origination is just another
word for growth.

Once we attend to its material, then, our wooden table no longer
figures as an object in the record. Rather, the record is in the object,
embedded in a material history of germination and growth. With a
kind of reverse archaeology, we excavate not to discover objects in the
record, but to find the record in objects. We could take our table, or
a large wooden beam, or even a fallen trunk, and cut away layer after
layer, guided by the rings of annual growth, to find nested within it
a series of ever more slender trees, right back to the initial sapling.

Within every tree hide ever-younger versions of itself. But the younger the versions, the older they are, in the sense that they have been there for longer. Contrariwise, the older the versions of the tree, the younger they are. That is why to dig into the tree is to undo the work of time. It is like running a film of the tree's growth, shot over decades, if not centuries, in fast reverse.

Art

The body is a solid form, bounded by the skin. Breath is of the air, flesh of the earth. Light casts a shadow when obstructed by an opaque object. We grasp a tree-trunk with our hand, but it feels nothing. Growth is irreversible. The surface of the skin, especially at the fingers and the lips, is sensitive to touch. Leaves blow in the wind. Thorns prick. These are some of the many things we tend to take for granted as we go about our daily lives. They are not necessarily wrong. But when they go without saying, as they generally do, we may fail to notice the more fundamental conditions upon which their truth depends. These are the very conditions of our existence in the world. And it stands to reason that our experience can only be enriched by paying attention to them.

One way of doing this is by way of experiments that would put everything we assume into reverse. What if the breath were solid, and what we take to be the body aerial? What if light swirled in the heavens like the wind, and shadows lay in piles of fallen leaves? What if, instead of grasping the tree, the tree had our hand in its grasp? What if we could reverse the flow of time, and cause trees to shrink? What if the wind were the breath of leaves, and the skin a bed of thorns? What do these experiments, and others like them, tell us about bodies, about the senses, about memory and time, about ourselves and the world in which we dwell?

They are certainly not scientific, these experiments. No data are extracted; no hypotheses put to the test. It is a principle of scientific objectivity that nature be held at arm's length; that the investigator should remain unmoved and unperturbed by the condition of phenomena under study. The pursuit of objectivity, however, should not be mistaken for the quest for truth. For while the former requires that we sever all connections with the world, the latter demands our full and unqualified participation. It impels us to open the world to our perception, to what is going on there, so that we in turn can answer to it. In so doing, we absorb into our own ways of working a perceptual acuity attuned to the materials that have captured our attention. As these materials vary, so does the experience that comes from working with them. Or in a word, materials and experience *correspond*. In his art, Giuseppe Penone corresponds with trees, bodies, the wind and much more; in this essay, I have tried something similar. I hope, thereby, to have brought my own, verbal correspondence into correspondence with his artistic one.

Ta, Da, Ça!

I wrote these lines in response to an intervention by the artist Émile Kirsch. Its title, Ta, Da, Ça!, *is drawn from the writings of philosopher-semiotician Roland Barthes, who attributes the phrase, in turn, to the Sanskrit* tathata, *literally translated as 'that, there it is, lo!'[1] Barthes imagines the small child, pointing at something and exclaiming, 'look, there!' The intervention itself requires only the most minimal apparatus: a set of tiny tubes of magnetized steel, each no more than one centimetre long and half a centimetre in diameter, open at one end but closed at the other by a circular flange. This little object will spontaneously cling, by the flat surface of the flange, to any artefacts susceptible to magnetic attraction, without leaving the slightest mark. But the open end of the tube affords a snug fit for twigs of roughly the right diameter. For* Ta, Da, Ça!, *Kirsch collected twigs from the woods to stick into his tubes, and proceeded to affix them to metal objects around the house and in the city. All of a sudden, twigs would sprout, indoors and out, from radiators, kitchen appliances, metal furniture, railings, drainpipes and road signs.* Ta, Da, Ça! *not only draws our attention to artefacts in our surroundings that we so often take for granted; it also playfully upends our conventional understanding of the order of things. Objects that we thought were complete, contained and domesticated appear to germinate, to grow, and to proliferate. A certain wildness sets in. Here I offer some thoughts stimulated by my own experiments with* Ta, Da, Ça! *What happens if we take twigs from their natural habitat in the woods and plant them in the artefactual environment of the city?*

Twig: 'a slender shoot issuing from a branch or stem'. The woods are full of twigs, and this pithy definition, extracted from the *Oxford*

English Dictionary, tells us all we need to know. Three things stand out in particular. First, when it comes to woody material, the twig is as thin as it gets. In the growing tree, it is the ultimate level of subdivision before finally giving way to bud or leaf. Secondly, the twig issues forth along a line of growth with no determinate end-point, improvising a passage with only one objective, namely to find a way into the light. And thirdly, it deviates. Whatever line the parent branch might take, the twig insists on taking another. The branch having already booked its place in the sun, the twig sets off in search of somewhere else. Yet every twig carries within it the potential for further deviation, becoming itself a branch in relation to its further offshoots. That is what gives rise to the characteristically irregular, forked structure of twigs that are serially divided. When we find them, scattered on a woodland floor, many forks are already snapped off, as are the twigs themselves from the branches which had once borne them. What had been a fork, then, becomes a sharp bend. Twigs are neither straight nor gracefully curved. They are always crooked.

Animals living in the woods know how to cope with the irregularity of twigs, and can even turn it to their advantage. For many birds, for example, twigs are ideal for nest building. They can be assembled into a structure that may be ragged at the edges, but nevertheless holds together in its disintegration, precisely because of the way every twig catches every other in its knots, forks and bends. The very looseness of the structure allows it to withstand the battering of the wind, as it rocks the boughs in which the nest is set. Humans, for their part, have learned from their observations of the accomplishments of animals, and in the arts of wicker-work have taken them to a new level, weaving or plaiting twigs into pens, traps, baskets, cradles, chairs and a host of other structures of everyday use. Moreover, in the home, bunches of twigs bound at one end, or tied to a staff, make brushes and brooms that are perfect for sweeping up stray material on rough, uneven surfaces. In every case, the utensils in question hold together through the springiness and friction of their entwined materials. Twigs are not naturally predisposed to fit together into larger structures – they are not, in that sense, parts of wholes. In its precise configuration, every twig is unique. Yet together, they can incline towards a kind of settlement.

We humans, however, are no longer at home in the woods as we once were. We have chosen, rather, to surround ourselves with objects of our own design, made by cutting, shaping and moulding materials into the forms of geometrically regular solids. These are our artefacts; and although the artefact may, in principle, be anything of human manufacture, in practice it is the formal properties of things, and their attribution to design, that single them out as artificial. As a designed object, the artefact is everything the twig is not. For its solidity does not arise incrementally, along a line of growth, but is already encased within the smooth and even facets of a form. Whereas the twig shoots uncontrollably every which way, the artefact is chunked, its interior having been blocked off from its exterior surroundings. One embodies principles of growth and deviation; the other the opposite principles of preformation and containment. For the former, the loose end is a sign of future growth and prosperity; for the latter it signals either unfinished business or disintegration. Perhaps no-one has put the contrast better than the Sophist author Antiphon, writing in the fifth century BCE. If you plant a wooden bed in the ground, Antiphon observed, it might take root and sprout new shoots. But what will come up will be fresh wood, not a new bed![2]

What we have, then, are two different and indeed incompatible orders: the vegetative and the artefactual. The vegetative order – the order of the twig – is constituted by the power of growth. The artefactual order is constituted by the power of the intellect, to impose its own designs on the material world. To this belong sundry manufactured objects. In the woods, the vegetative order prevails. Everything sprouts. If artefacts are there at all, they are lost or adrift, perhaps accidentally dropped by passers-by. But in town, it is the twiggy things that are now on the back foot. Even wicker-work has become an anachronism. Your besom of twigs, finding no purchase on the smooth surfaces of the artefactual assemblage, has been replaced by the vacuum cleaner. Everything is encased; nothing sprouts. Can these two orders be joined in conviviality? At first glance this looks implausible. For if twiggy things are knotted through the deviation and entwinement of their singular elements, the integrity of artefacts depends on an interlocking in which every piece finds its place as part of a larger whole. A twig can find nothing in the order of artefacts on which to bind; conversely, an artefact has no shoots with which to attach itself to vegetation. But perhaps the division is not really so stark. Could things of all sorts be both solidified into chunks and frayed at the edges?

The question is of how things are joined. Even in a world of artefacts, nothing is a perfect fit. Things have to be fastened by means of glue, clips, springs, pins, screws and plugs of various descriptions. Common to all is that they compromise the integrity of the bounding surfaces of objects. Most glues, for example, are formed of long protein molecules that can penetrate the surfaces to which they are applied, effectively binding them together. For a surface that looks integral to the naked eye is, at the molecular level, more like a sieve. It is full of holes. Clips and springs work thanks to the elasticity of the materials from which they are made: to their capacity to be bent out of form and their inclination to return to it. Pins puncture surfaces, but screws do more, as the thread of the screw bites into the very flesh of the material and pulls it tight. And plugs, albeit precisely cut to fit their sockets, are held in place by forces of friction equivalent to the strength required to push them in. Finally, there remains the possibility of magnetism, thanks to which one metal object can lock onto another, without even puncturing its surface. For as with gravity, the attraction of the magnet is of one interior mass to another, irrespective of the outward forms they assume (Figure 5).

It takes only a little thing to scratch the surface of the artefactual world and, in so doing, to release the vegetative power of materials from their artefactual case and restore the city to the woods. Bury the objects, and the city – like Antiphon's bed – begins to sprout. Delicate and slender lines of growth are observed to poke out from its surfaces, tentatively seeking a way into the light, forking as they go.

Figure 5 *Ta, Da, Ça!* (stick, magnet, radiator), photo by Émile Kirsch, 2017. (Courtesy of the artist.)

Inhabitants stop to wonder at it. They are astonished. What can it portend? 'We are used to our city's being always under construction,' they say, 'but not to twigs sprouting from pipes and radiators, road signs and railings. Is this a city or a forest?' That is the question of *Ta, Da, Ça!*

SPITTING, CLIMBING, SOARING, FALLING

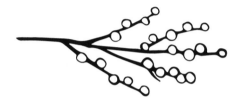

Introduction

In a tale from medieval Ireland, told by Bishop Patrick of Dublin in the eleventh century and retold by the poet Seamus Heaney in the twentieth, worshippers at prayer espied a ship floating in the sky, whence descended an anchor rope. The anchor itself, having snagged on a rail of the altar, had brought the ship to a juddering halt. A crewman shinnied down the rope to try to free it, but could not. Realizing that the man was close to drowning, the abbot ordered his congregation to help. The anchor was eventually released and – in the nick of time – the crewman made it back up the rope to rejoin his ship, which sailed on out of sight.[1]

The medium of air we mortals breathe to stay alive was, for the celestial seafarer, a death-trap. It would have killed him, had it not been for the abbot's timely intervention. Would the salty sea not kill us too, were we to spend too long beneath the waves? On land as at sea, we humans must have air to breathe. We live, necessarily, beneath the sky, on or at the surfaces formed where earth, air and water meet and mingle. There are surfaces where water meets air: such are the waves, whipped up by wind and ocean currents. But there are also surfaces, of the ground, where air meets earth, and of the sea-floor, where earth meets water. Air is above water; water above earth. Are people living on the earth, then, living underwater? That's how it must have seemed to the ghostly mariners of Patrick's story. But for the congregation below, their ship appeared to sail the dome of the sky itself. It was a ship of heaven. For from the point of view of God's heaven, as St Augustine had observed, the sky belongs to the material earth of His creation, an earth that also includes its lands and oceans.[2]

Yet our ships, too, would appear celestial to the denizens of the deep, and many must have wondered at the strange things fallen from this heavenly realm: chests of gold, cannon shot, anchor chains and, of course, human beings, drowning if not already dead. Today, more than ever, the oceans are filling with the residues of human life on land, whether cast overboard from shipping, washed down by the flood, or carried as dust by offshore winds. But what the sea receives, it also spits up again, and it is from here – at the water's edge where waves pound the shore – that we commence our journey in the four essays to follow. Venturing inland, we begin to climb, rising higher and higher, into hills and mountains, in the ultimately vain attempt to attain a God's-eye view. Taking off with the birds, we soar into the sky, sailing over mountaintops like a balloon. But being mortal, we are fated, finally, to fall back to earth, just as water vapour, forced upwards by rising elevations, must eventually condense and fall as rain or snow.

The foamy saliva of a horse

New Year's Day, 2016, found me walking the beach along which the city of Aberdeen, where I live, faces the North Sea. Ten days of relentless rain and easterly gales had brought misery to many whose homes lay too close to the raging rivers Dee and Don, whose estuaries bound the city, respectively, to the south and to the north. Dwellings were flooded, roads underwater, bridges destroyed. An entire caravan park had been washed away; with it went not just people's belongings but the memories of countless holidays, all hurtling tumultuously down the rivers and into the sea. The city itself had survived relatively unscathed. On the beach, however, the sight that greeted my eyes was like nothing I had ever seen before. It was not just the sea that foamed, as though mightily angered by some cosmic insult. The sandy beach itself was buried under a foot-deep coating of off-white spume that seemed spookily alive as it writhed in the wind, sending its airborne flecks inland. It was odd and strangely disconcerting to tread in this material: light as air, and offering no resistance, it nevertheless lapped around one's feet like an ooze that threatened at any moment to swallow one up. As I picked my way through the spume, I was reminded of an exhibition I had seen a couple of years previously, at Glasgow's Common Guild gallery, of work by the artist and sculptor Carol Bove. The exhibition had been entitled The Foamy Saliva of a Horse.

What could Bove have meant by this enigmatic title? No explanation was provided. There was no horse in the show, and no saliva. On further investigation I came across a legend according to which Apelles, court painter to Alexander the Great in the fourth century BCE, was once so enraged by his failure to depict the foaming saliva of a panting horse that he took the sponge with which he would clean his brushes and threw it at the picture. Instantly, the desired effect was achieved. Some five centuries later, this story reappeared in the writings of the Graeco-Roman physician Sextus Empiricus. He used it to illustrate the predicament of the sceptical philosopher, equally tormented by his inability to decide between objects of sense, on the one hand, and objects of thought, on the other. The sceptic's response, according to Sextus, should be simply to suspend judgement – to throw in the sponge, as we might say – and let chance decide. In that state of suspension, the philosopher finds release from torment and a certain peace of mind. Could this, then, be the clue to what Bove was doing in her art? What happens when the neat, crystalline lattice of our conceptions comes up against the exuberance and excess of a world of life and death, of growth and decomposition? Can they be suspended in some kind of balance? And can this balance restore a sense of tranquillity amidst the turmoil of the elements?

The exhibition was on two floors. One of the works on the upper floor comprised a vertical metal stand, set upon a rectangular plinth, equipped with branches and hooks which supported a variety of sea shells. In themselves, the shells are objects of great beauty (Figure 6). But they have not been made; they are not artefacts. Like soap bubbles caught in suspension, their rounded forms owe nothing to human thought and everything to the mathematics of growth. The linear stand, by contrast, owes everything to thought. With its branches and hooks, it is a three-dimensional diagram that sets the shells in relation to one another as part of a scheme, perhaps taxonomic, perhaps morphological. In the diagram, the objects of sense (the shells) are both suspended in, and supported by, an object of thought (the stand). That's upstairs, above sea-level, so to speak. Downstairs, set upon a mantelpiece, I found a similar stand, and similar shells. But all bar one of the shells had apparently fallen from the stand and lay scattered on the mantelpiece (Figure 7). Below sea-level, it seems, the turbulence of the world wins out over our efforts to contain it, and things will not conform to our conceptual delineations. It turned out that this contrast between above and below, between oversea

Figure 6 Sea shells on stand, from Carol Bove, *The Foamy Saliva of a Horse*. (© Carol Bove, 2011. Courtesy of the Ovitz Family Collection, Los Angeles. Photo by Lorenzo Vitturi.)

and undersea, established a frame for the entire exhibition. But it also gave another clue to its title. The foamy saliva of a horse? It is of course a riddle of the sea.

Every horse is a wave, tipped with foam, and the exhibition was about the things the white horses of the sea spit up upon the shore. Over countless centuries, the ocean has swallowed up things of human

Figure 7 Sea shells off stand, from Carol Bove, *The Foamy Saliva of a Horse.* (© Carol Bove, 2011. Courtesy of the Ovitz Family Collection, Los Angeles. Photo by Lorenzo Vitturi.)

manufacture and – after varying lengths of time – spat them up again. Tossed from the foam of a raging sea, the wreckage of tanks, drums, nets and decomposing timbers is spread before our eyes. In the very processes of corrosion, and of battering by the elements, once clean-cut artefacts can take on weird and wonderful forms, and their surfaces – originally polished to a reflective sheen that would have hidden the noxious substances that lay beneath or within – become like the surface of the earth itself: infinitely variegated, multi-textured, composite and reactive. This is what had happened to a rusty oil drum which Bove had found and exhibited. As new, it had taken the form of a perfect cylinder, straight in elevation and circular in section. Its shiny, painted surface would have given no hint of the slick it contained. The visible exterior and invisible interior were kept absolutely separate. Now, however, long since relieved of its contents, the drum's contorted surface embraces the outside like the folds of a fabric, while particles of rust, in the process of detaching themselves, or already detached and scattered around, attest to the gradual disintegration of the boundary between surface and medium.

One further piece in the exhibition, also placed downstairs, speaks of an oceanic struggle between nature and artifice. A massive block of driftwood, standing on end, slightly askew, could once have been a pillar for a groyne. One of the bolts still remains, emerging from one side, by which the cladding it supported would have been affixed. This timber would have stood fast against the sea, breaking the force of its surge, and holding in place the sediment of sand and shingle beneath. But it could not resist forever, and perhaps in the violence of a storm it could no longer withstand, it was washed away. Thereafter, its fortunes were reversed, for now the block that once broke the sea is at its mercy, tossed by white horses, only to be spat ashore in its foamy saliva. In the sea this massive block, far too heavy for a man to lift, would have been floatingly light. Back on earth, once again heavy and lethargic, it tells of its journeys in the gnarling, knotting and scouring of its flesh, in which the grain is very clearly revealed. Not only that, but the smell and blackened surfaces tell that it had once been coated with bitumen. And it was the recollection of this item in the exhibit that brought me back, with a jolt, to where I stood, on Aberdeen beach. For there I was, surrounded on all sides by the foamy saliva of a horse.

The entire beach is lined with groynes. Although they had survived the storm intact, the groynes had also snagged what the sea had thrown up, preventing it from washing back. Whole trees uprooted, massive timbers, and branches festooned with grass lay strewn across the beach, some of them perched perilously on the groynes as if they had been tossed about like matchsticks (Figure 8). And then there were the supermarket trolleys. Along with discarded shoes and the ubiquitous plastic bric-à-brac, metal drums and car tyres, the trolleys were the most abundant of the debris of human manufacture. Most of them looked as if they had been submerged for years. Though much of what was cast up, including heaps of withered grass, had clearly come down the rivers to the sea, only to be thrown back on shore by

Figure 8 Groynes on Aberdeen beach. A tree-trunk, tossed up by the storm of New Year, 2016, remains, four years later, snagged between the pillars. (Photo by the author.)

the violence of the waves, it was clear that the population of drums, tyres and trolleys was not new to the watery environment. They had perhaps spent more time underwater than they had above it. But cast up on the beach, the wreckage of human concepts, and their artefactual embodiments, seemed to find some repose, and even to take on a kind of beauty, half-buried in sand or nestled in the branches of washed-up trees.

Observing the scene, I was not alone. Many citizens had been drawn to the beach by the same curiosity as mine, and were picking their way through the debris in a trance-like state of amazement, accompanied by their fiercely investigative dogs, while sea-birds wheeled as if they had never had it so good. I wondered, as I roamed the beach, whether I was looking into the city of the future, a city in which the opposition between the *polis* and the ocean, as old as Plato, has finally succumbed to the inevitability of rising sea-levels. For more than two millennia we have striven to keep the two apart, and to preserve the order of the city, governed by reason, from the tumult of the sea, which threatens its dissolution. Even now, there are cities in which the battle is being lost – Venice being the most celebrated example – while victory, it seems, can never be more than provisional and calls for ever more massive and improbable feats of engineering. At some point, like the sceptic Sextus Empiricus, we will have to raise the white flag and seek a reconciliation between the rule of abstract reason and the material tumult of the weather-world in which we are fated to live. Can the city ever make its peace with the sea? Or could we be entering an era in which cities become oceans, on which their buildings float like ships?

The mountaineer's lament

In November 2014, Deveron Arts – an arts organization based in the town of Huntly, in rural Aberdeenshire – staged a two-day symposium in the little town of Tomintoul, perched high in the Cairngorm hills.[1] *The symposium was attended by local people, hillwalkers, a number of artists, an anthropologist (myself) and one world-famous mountaineer, specially invited for the occasion. The hillwalkers and artists spoke with enthusiasm about their exploration of the highlands, following familiar tracks and trails. Immersed as they were in the landscape, they found in it a source of perpetual astonishment: the ever-changing skies, the play of light, shadow and colour, the comings and goings of animals, the sprouting and flowering of plants, intriguing stones and rock formations, even the occasional archaeological find attesting to the long history of human habitation of the region. There was always something to catch one's attention, and to pursue further.*

But when it was the mountaineer's turn to speak, the mood abruptly changed, from celebration to despondency. Here was a man who had been among the first to conquer some of the highest and most challenging peaks on earth. His audience listened spellbound as he entertained them with tales of breath-taking exploits, of exploration and discovery, illustrated by slides which predominantly featured panoramic shots of formidable landforms or close-ups of men in gear and goggles. Yet he spoke not in triumph but in sorrow. For now that every mountain peak had been conquered, many by the man himself, short of starting afresh on another planet, the only future for exploration, he thought, lay underground, in a kind of upside-down mountaineering that would carry the torch of humanity to ever greater depths rather than to the most ascendant heights. 'There are no explorers any more,' he lamented, 'only cavers!'

For me, the great man's remark set so many discordant bells ringing that I paid scant attention to the rest of what he had to say. How could it be, I wondered, that while the hillwalkers and artists could keep on exploring, without end, the mountaineer was convinced that it was all over? What leads him, and us, to believe that a mountain climbed once has been climbed for ever? What does this say about our understandings of perception, imagination and memory? Indeed this one remark seemed to harbour within it a whole agenda for thinking about what mountains really are, why they fascinate or repel, how they play on our conceptions of humanity and what it means to be alive, how we experience earth, sky and the ground between them, and how we measure up – in distance and altitude – the space of human habitation.

We all come into the world as infants, so let us start from there. For every infant, the world that gradually opens up to their perception is a fount of continual wonder. The allure of everything and every-one around them motivates them to get moving, by whatever means are available, in order to discover more. Infants and small children are compulsive explorers, and are making discoveries all the time. Nor do they have to venture far from home to do so. Indeed they are more likely to discover things close to home, where familiarity affords the freedom to wander about in relative safety, unshackled by straps, harnesses and other protective gear. As grown-ups, however, we are convinced that everything within the circle of the familiar is already known, and that to explore we must go further, expand our horizons, and gear ourselves up – mentally as well as physically – for the challenge. The adult's sense of exploration, it seems, is the precise opposite of the child's. One, the child's, is centripetal; the other, the adult's, is centrifugal. For young children, perception and imagina-tion are one, not because their world is one of fantasy rather than fact, but because they are themselves immersed in the process of things becoming what they are. Everything and everyone has – or, rather, *is* – their own story, their own way of becoming, and the child-explorer, going on her way, joins her story with theirs in a correspondence that can continue for as long as life goes on. The familiar world, for the child, is an inexhaustible source of revelation. Adults, by contrast, understand their world to be complete and fully formed. To convert imagination into reality, or fantasy into fact, they therefore have to go beyond the limits of the already known. This is what drives the would-be adult explorer ever further afield.

Is there some point, then, in the life-cycle of a human being when childlike exploration ends and adult exploration begins? Or is it rather that as we get older, a certain discourse – shot through with idioms of territoriality, conquest and the human domination of nature – exerts an increasing grip on the mind? In this discourse there are two sorts of exploration, and two sorts of discovery. The first establishes a curriculum, in the form of a condensed recapitulation of past human achievements, that every child is expected to follow in the course of their education. In this adultocentric conception of learning, children are merely playing catch-up on their predecessors, discovering for themselves what earlier generations already knew, climbing mountains they had climbed. The second is the sort of exploration and discovery of which we pretend that never in all of human history has it been done or made before. Here the explorer-discoverer – commonly assumed to be male – takes the first step, pulling the rest of humanity in his wake. From these small steps, we say, is the history of humankind made. This imagination of history, I believe, lay behind the lament of the regretful mountaineer. If making history means setting foot where no man has been before, then how can human history continue if there are no more summits on which to stand for the first time? The great man seemed almost to be offering an apology for the fact that he had bagged so many mountains for himself, leaving none for future generations. Are we now condemned to the endless recapitulation of a once glorious past? Is the inverse mountaineering of the caver the only remaining option, or would we do better to direct our ambition to other planets? Might there be mountains to be climbed on Mars?

In the narrative of territorial conquest, peaks imagined are progressively converted into peaks remembered; the eye-witness account paints the mountain as a *true story*, a thing of fact rather than fiction.

But to paint it thus is also to deny the mountain any story of its own. To say that, once climbed, every subsequent climb is a repeat performance is to assume that the mountain itself remains exactly as it was – that while history moves on, the mountain is on the side of an ever-constant nature. But nature is not constant. As the philosopher Alfred North Whitehead once observed, 'there is no holding nature still and looking at it.'[2] Mountains have their stories just as we do. A peak that had never seen a human before our mountaineer arrived has, since then, seen many more humans. They have built steps in its gullies, hammered spikes into its rock faces, left their litter all over the place. But for a mountain that has been shaped over aeons of time by earthquakes and eruptions, by immense forces of descending ice and water, and by extremes of weather, the human imprint must seem of little consequence. For the great slumbering giant, the conquering hero is no more than a minor irritant, like a fly on the tip of its nose. The mountain does not feel conquered or domesticated, contacted by civilization or incorporated into the human fold. It promptly forgets – if it ever noticed – that someone was up there, waving his arms ecstatically on the summit. It just goes on being there, doing its thing. Indigenous people, for whom mountains are a familiar, everyday presence, know to treat them with respect. They have often ascended their mountains many times, long before explorers arrived to climb them 'for the first time', not in order to claim them for themselves, but to petition for their protection and prosperity, for clement weather and good crops.

In the sixth century BCE, the Greek philosopher Heraclitus is alleged to have declared that you cannot step twice into the same waters of a flowing river. Is it not the same with the mountain? Is not every ascent the first? This depends on how you define the mountain. Perhaps you will identify it as the landform seen from afar, with its characteristic profile. 'Here is a picture of Everest,' you say; 'Everest is a mountain.' It looks like a mountain because you are far away from it. Any profile, of course, will be one of many, often markedly different, viewed from different vantage points. But they all add up to a monumental presence which gives every sign of permanence.

Having once been climbed for the first time, then every subsequent climb of the same mountain is a repeat performance. The only way to introduce variation is by changing the route, tackling this face rather than that. But for the climber on the slopes or at the summit, the mountain is not a profile, nor even a route. Indeed it doesn't really look like a mountain at all. It rather feels like one. And that feeling is one of immersion in a whole that comprises the rock and earth beneath one's feet, the sky above, and between them the carpet of vegetation, the waters of bubbling brooks and stagnant bog, birds and beasts, rain and snow, clouds and swirling mists. Here you are climbing, to be sure, but you are not climbing the mountain. Rather, you are climbing *in* the mountain. What is more, you can never climb twice in the same mountain. For if the mountain is all flow, then – just as Heraclitus observed for the river – the idea that a mountain ascended once is ascended forever is simply absurd.

So when the regretful mountaineer told us that all peaks have been climbed, and that none remain to be conquered, it can only be because he understood the mountain from the perspective of one who is not *in* it. He does not inhabit the mountain but goes at it as a soldier might embark on a campaign, fitting himself up against a perceived adversary and hoping to prevail by force of arms. And then he leaves, having reached the summit and secured his place in history. This explains why his pictures are either distant shots with no people in them, or close-ups with people armed to the teeth and laden with equipment. For inhabitants, mountains are part of a familiar but ever-evolving world, where nothing is the same from one moment to the next. Inhabitants get to know this world by making paths through it. Life is measured out in steps and traced along the ground. The mountaineer, however, is not an inhabitant but an occupant. His lines are not traced in walking but are first projected, as a solution to the puzzle of how to get from base to summit by a connected sequence of points, and then enacted on site by means of ropes and spikes. Paradoxically, this places the most distant peaks closer to metropolitan centres from which every expedition typically starts, than to the inhabited rural areas in the foothills. The mountaineer's telescopic vision vaults the hills to reach the summits, the angles of which are framed in the distant view. The lands in-between are merely to be passed through; their inhabitants maybe pressed into service as porters for the expedition's baggage. Even today, mountaineers tell of their exploits as if the odd sighting of a local person going about their business, perhaps herding animals or cutting hay on steep inclines, were an irrelevance.

People, in the practice of their livelihood, go along. But the mountaineer has only one aim, to go up. His ambition is framed by verticality. For him it is the summit that counts, not the great, heaving mass of rock of which the summit just happens to be the highpoint. If you are a farmer or a herdsman, or even a traveller, and if you are more interested in making your way through a landscape than in rising to the top, then do not call it a mountain. Call it a hill! Where mountains are for climbing, hills are for walking. Though climbers tend to speak of hills rather disdainfully, as landforms of insufficient stature to qualify as proper mountains, the real difference comes down to the question of how the relation between land and form, or ground and feature, is understood. The walker, whether going uphill, downhill or on the level, remains in continuous contact with the ground by way of the feet. Thus the ground itself appears corrugated, and the hills and valleys are its folds. These corrugations are felt in the muscles, whether straining with or against the force of gravity. Not so for the mountaineer, however. From his telescopic perspective, the ground figures as an isotropic plane, open to the horizon and level with the sea, upon which are placed forms and features as if on a base. The earth itself appears furnished, and among its furniture, mountains are by far the biggest and most impressive features. In this perception, the mountain is not ground but a structure that rises from it, with base, sides and top. As the climber scales the mountainsides, so he pulls himself ever further up. Whereas hillwalking is a way of inhabiting the world, or a practice of immanence, what the mountain offers the occupant climber is transcendence. And for that, he is prepared to risk life and limb.

On flight

In the Andes of southwestern Bolivia lies the world's most extensive salt flat, Salar de Uyuni. When covered with a thin layer of water, the flat becomes a mirror that perfectly reflects the sky. As the artist Tomás Saraceno found, to walk the flat under these conditions feels like floating among the clouds, during daylight hours, or among the stars, at night. This feeling inspired him to imagine an epoch in which the air, and not the earth, would be the primary medium of habitation. He called it the Aerocene. Fuelled only by sunlight, lifted by currents of warm air, or suspended from filaments as fine as spiders' webs, life in the Aerocene would be lightweight and delicate. Borne by the wind, it would afford complete freedom of movement, unconstrained by borders. In pursuit of his vision, and with a growing community of supporters around the world, Saraceno has been collecting waste plastic bags, and assembling them into vast balloons that have already broken records for solar-powered flight. The following essay was commissioned for a volume to celebrate the coming epoch. It was published in 2017.[1]

It is perhaps appropriate that I am writing this essay on board a plane. It is a commercial airliner, on a scheduled flight from London to Chicago. I am flying, so it says in the *High Life* magazine that I find in the seat pocket, courtesy of the company that operates the plane. Yet nothing feels less like flying to me. I am cocooned inside a machine that weighs hundreds of tons, strapped to a seat that restrains my movement to a wiggling of the toes, and breathing air that circulates the breath of my fellow passengers while remaining hermetically sealed from the atmosphere outside. I find I have become a fiercely territorial animal, defending every centimetre of my armrest and tray table against the incursions of my surly neighbour and his ever-unravelling newspaper. At least I have a window seat, affording a vision of the earth below. We are passing over northwest England, and down there I suppose there are people leading lives not unlike the one I led until, only an hour or two ago, I boarded the plane. Yet I can have no connection with them, not even as fleeting as the wave that one might hazard to onlookers from a passing train. The bafflement, no doubt, is reciprocated: how often, from my own home, have I watched a plane passing high overhead, its fuselage glinting in the sun and painting the sky with its vapour trail, and marvelled that inside such a distant object – so remote, so mysterious – there might be people like me, perhaps enjoying their dinner or, more probably, defending their little patches of seating space? Whence came the strange idea that life could be thus packaged up, encapsulated and despatched to points across the surface of the globe?

Don't get me wrong. An airliner is a marvellous thing, an object of beauty, a triumph of the techno-scientific imagination and a testament to the extraordinary twentieth-century history of aviation – a history that has combined ingenuity, endurance and courage with incendiary violence on a previously unimaginable scale. I am thankful that the plane I am on will get me safely to my destination within hours (else you will not be reading this), where in olden times I would have had to suffer weeks at sea followed by a treacherous journey overland. My argument is not against airliners. It is rather against the idea that airliners can fly, or that people can fly in them. Yes: they get off the ground. And yes: they are propelled through the air. But the same might be said of many other things, from cricket balls to cannon shot, most of which come under the general category of missiles. And after 9/11, we hardly need reminding that the airliner, too, can be a missile. The trajectory of the missile is determined by a compound of the force of gravity and the thrust and direction of propulsion. It may be guided by feedback from a target. But to fly is not to surrender to such mechanical determinations, nor is it to draw an arc from a point of origin to a destination. It is rather to find one's way, and one's being, amidst the currents and circulations of atmospheric air.

Flying, in short, is not mechanical; it is existential. Birds fly, because to *be* a bird is at once to be a bird-of-the-air. The same is true of other winged creatures, from flying insects to bats. No doubt it was once true of pterodactyls.

Whether it is or has ever been true of humans, however, is moot. It is often said that human beings cannot fly unaided, simply because – as the wise but supercilious Owl reminded Winnie-the-Pooh, in A. A. Milne's immortal fable – they lack the necessary dorsal muscles. Pooh, it will be recalled, had recourse to a balloon, with which he planned to rise into the air and negotiate with the bees, in the hope of obtaining some of their honey. He thought he could actually become an aerial being, akin to a cloud, though the bees – very much to his discomfiture – thought otherwise. Perhaps the closest most of us come to flying is in our dreams, in which we *become bird*, not as a thing of flesh and feathers but as a composition of air and movement in which the dreamer is borne aloft and carried along.[2] Flight is the feeling of airborne life, untethered. But I wonder whether we might nevertheless fly even without losing our earthly bearings, in quotidian life as much as in our dreams. Sometimes, when walking in a strong wind, and especially on high ground, we feel as if we are flying, and perhaps we are. It is an exhilarating experience. There is no doubt that I feel much closer to the birds, and to the experience of flying, when walking in the hills than when seated on this plane. So why should we say – as we usually do on such occasions – that we are walking and *not* flying? Why cannot we do both at once? Are not our heaving lungs as much in communion with the swirling air as are our plodding feet with the earth? Does not breath follow breath as step follows step?

Maybe we should regard walking as two-legged flying: a way of flying that has yet to take off. Indeed flying in this sense bears some comparison with sailing. While the hull of the vessel skims the waves, its sails catch the wind: it is as much airborne as waterborne. Thus sailing, too, could be the mariner's way of flying. And although the analogy might seem far-fetched, I just wonder whether the same might be said of writing, at least as it was practised in ages before the advent of the printed word. Medieval scribes often drew parallels between their writing and the passage of a wayfarer through the terrain, and between the letter-line traced by the pen and the path traced by feet. Could writing have been the scribe's way of flying, as walking was the pedestrian's way? Don't forget that the scribe would have used a quill pen, made from a feather that had once graced a bird on the wing. Thanks to this feather, it is now the writer's hand that flies, so as to leave its sinuous trace on the page. Perhaps the parallel between writing and flying is even more apparent in the oriental traditions of brush calligraphy, which often took inspiration from the flight of birds and the wispy forms of clouds. Here, the flying brush skims the paper, leaving its traces like passing eddies of wind in the dust of dry ground. The walker's lines, the mariner's lines and the writer's lines, let us say, are all *lines of flight*, and what is characteristic of such lines is not just that they are aerial, but that they escape the determinations of origin and target. They go not from A to B but through the midst of things. It is no accident that 'to flee' and 'to fly' are etymologically cognate, and that both conjugate to 'flight'.

Today, of course, the writer is typically no longer a scribe or a calligrapher but a wordsmith, whose verbal compositions are committed to page or screen by means of a mechanism. Yet we still call the typed or printed document a 'manuscript', *as if* its lines were drawn in the flight of the hand. The same wishful anachronism is at work when we speak of the flight of the airliner, or the sailing of its ocean-going counterpart. Just as it is impossible to write – in the original sense of scribing or tracing a line – with a keyboard, so, strictly speaking, it is not possible to fly with the plane or to sail with the ship. The liner's line does indeed go from A to B. The ship, with its propellers, drills through the ocean as though making a hole through which it can pass, much as the airliner – once equipped with propellers but now with jet engines – bores its way through the sky. In one case water, in the other air, is both a medium and a resistance to be overcome, and this is done by using an external power source to induce a turbulence that is foreign to its nature. But the fish in the water and the bird in the air operate quite differently. Their bodies, equipped, respectively, with fins and wings, are designed to move not *against* the medium but *with* it, coupling their own energies with its fluid dynamics. Water for the fish and air for the bird is not a homogeneous mass through which one has relentlessly to drill, as does the tunneller through solid rock, but a highly differentiated texture, woven by materials in motion to create the eddies and thermals that denizens of the ocean and the sky can both harness and inflect to their advantage.

Looking out from my passenger window, I can see something of this texture in the formations of clouds that currently blanket the earth. It is otherwise invisible to us. Yet birds can feel it, and so I suppose can glider pilots and balloonists. I regret that I have never flown in either a glider or a balloon. Nor have I ever dropped to earth in a parachute, flown a microlight or indulged in the sport of skydiving. I therefore have little authority to write on these matters, and must rely on the testimony of others. One account comes from the artist Peter Lanyon, who took up gliding in 1959 as a way to enrich his previous practice of landscape painting. Lanyon had this to say of one of his most extraordinary works, *Thermal*, painted a year later (Figure 9): 'The air is a very definite world of activity as complex and demanding as the sea. The thermal itself is a current of hot air rising and eventually condensing into cloud. It is invisible and can only be apprehended by an instrument such as a glider. The basic source of all soaring flight is the thermal.'[3] But the painting not only references gliding. It also describes the flight of sea-birds as they negotiate the cliffs. They, too, must ride the complex currents that the wind sets up as it scours the rock-face. Or it could reference the predatory hawk which, having risen on the upward current, must strain muscle and sinew to hold a position directly above a location on the ground, preparing to swoop on unsuspecting prey. At last relaxing, it soars away on the wind. What looks like stillness for us is motion for the hawk, and, conversely, what we see as motion is the hawk's way of staying still.

It is the same for balloonists, who, up aloft, report an overwhelming sense of stillness. Precisely because the craft is moving with and not against the wind, it is as though one were becalmed. Down below, people might be holding on to their hats, but up above, all is quiet. Below, the wind wants to tear you away; above, you float in it. Stillness,

Figure 9 *Thermal*, 1960, by Peter Lanyon (1918–1964).
(Courtesy of the Tate Gallery, St Ives. © Estate of Peter Lanyon.
All Rights Reserved, DACS 2020.)

in short, is the perfect condition of movement, when all its elements are in harmony. We alight here on a profound truth, first enunciated by the Graeco-Sicilian philosopher Empedocles in the fifth century BCE. The cosmos, according to Empedocles, is formed through the perpetual dialogue of two opposed principles, which he named Love and Strife. Love, in its purest form, is spherical. Within the sphere, all the elements are in accord with one another; only at its surrounding surface does Strife come into play. But it is Strife that – by tearing the elements apart, mixing them and forming new combinations thereof – gives rise to all the material phenomena that we observe around us. In his time, Empedocles appealed to mythology to give body to his principles, in the figures of Aphrodite and Ares, deities respectively of Love and of Strife. Had he, however, been alive in the pioneering days of balloon flight, in the eighteenth and nineteenth centuries, he might well have seen in the balloon the perfect embodiment of Love, and in the force of the wind that would fain pull it from its moorings the epitome of Strife. But on a smaller scale, one has only to attend to the lowly soap bubble, all stillness and harmony within but bounded by the forces of surface tension in the liquid medium. Eventually and inevitably, Strife prevails, the bubble bursts: its liquid falls to earth and its inner breath vanishes into air.

Here I am on board an airliner, reflecting on stillness! It is paradoxical. I may be sitting perfectly still, with my seat-belt properly fastened in case of unexpected turbulence – those disconcerting moments when powerful atmospheric forces shake our confidence in the homogeneity of the medium – but I am chronically restless. I have an urge to move my limbs but cannot, and feel the stillness as a restraint. This is Strife, not Love. I want to get from London to Chicago as quickly as possible, and the time it takes is a measure of my impatience. Ideally, it should take no time at all. But then I soothe my restless mind with thoughts of floating bubbles, of dandelion clocks wafting on a summer's day, of stray particles of dust lit by sunbeams. Pictures of all of these, and more, may be found in the advertising pages of *High Life* magazine, which promise a utopia of peace and relaxation at journey's end – conditional, of course, on the payment of large sums of money. These pictures only reinforce the sense of inaccessibility, yet they appeal precisely because they resonate with real experience and pleasing memories. Yes: my attention, too, has, on occasion, wandered with soap bubbles and dandelion clocks, and in those moments I have felt the sense of stillness, and of harmony, that Empedocles described as Love. But then, this stillness is not an absence of movement. Absolute immobility would be tantamount to death. A living body has to breathe, its heart has to beat; blood has to circulate in its veins. We experience stillness when these bodily rhythms are in tune with the movements around us. That is why the hawk is still as it soars on the thermal, why fish are still as they dart about in the water, why the balloon is still as it drifts wherever the wind will take it, and why I am still as my attention remains rapt in the floating bubble – until it bursts.

These are the stillnesses of being alive, of harmonic sound rather than enforced silence. They are stillnesses that are held in movement, rather than striving against it. In his prose poem *De Rerum Natura* ('On the Nature of Things'), composed around 50 BCE, the Roman philosopher Titus Lucretius Carus put this in a nutshell:

> Herein wonder not
> how 'tis that, while the seeds of things are all
> Moving forever, the sum yet seems to stand
> Supremely still.[4]

Lucretius was a great admirer of Empedocles, and even used Empedocles' poem *On Nature* as a model for his own exposition. But for Lucretius the cosmos, in its purest or most pristine form, was not spherical but rectilinear. It was made up of innumerable atoms, perpetually raining down in parallel through the infinitude of space. Yet they have only to swerve a little in their course to collide with one another, and it is in the cascading of these collisions that a world is formed, consisting of endless permutations and combinations of matter. But we see the forms and not the flow, Lucretius argued: the world to us seems still even though it is entirely suspended in movement. Now listen to the philosopher Henri Bergson, writing a couple of millennia later, in the early twentieth century:

> Like eddies of dust raised by the wind as it passes, the living turn upon themselves, borne up by the great blast of life. They are therefore relatively stable, and counterfeit immobility so well that

we treat each of them as a thing rather than as a progress, forgetting that the very permanence of their form is only the outline of
a movement.[5]

Bergson is with Lucretius in thinking that life in general is given in
movement, and moreover in his conviction that for there to be particular living things it is necessary for this movement to veer from a course
that would otherwise be absolutely straight. But unlike Lucretius, he
saw the movement as going ever upwards, not downwards. Bergson
was writing at a time when balloon flight was in its heyday, and it is
quite possible that in writing of the 'great blast of life', he had the hot
air balloon in mind.

But what of myself, aboard this airliner? I am borne up, to be
sure, not, however, by the blast of life but by the blast of jet engines
burning fossil fuel. And my immobility is not so much the outline of a
movement as the product of its constriction. I am cocooned in a blast
of death, projected towards my destination in a guided missile, while
I dream of bubbles and dandelion clocks . . . until rudely awakened
by the thud of wheels on tarmac. My plane has landed. I stagger off to
join an immigration queue. Maybe, once I am out of the terminal and
back into the open air, I can begin to fly!

Sounds of snow

As climatic change threatens to turn cold-weather phenomena that were once commonplace into rarities, are we in danger of losing the vocabulary to describe them? This question took the artist Mikel Nieto, a native of the Basque Country, to winter in Finland, both to record the sounds of snow, and to link them to the many different words, in the Finnish language, for its different states and qualities. Nieto invited me to contribute an essay for a book, entitled A Soft Hiss of This World, *to accompany the project, and I readily accepted.[1] The book was printed in white letters on a white background, as if its letters and words had fallen silently like snowflakes onto the page. They could only be read in a certain light. In this essay, I reflect on the sounds of snow, and on how they figure in language, both Finnish and Scots.*

Have you ever heard a snowflake? Is every snowflake a sound? It's not like a raindrop. The drop surrenders its form when it hits the ground, and that's what we hear. If it falls in a puddle or a lake, it makes a little plop, actually the sound of another drop momentarily forming on the rebound. If it falls on grass or leaves, it trickles and runs. If it falls on paved ground, it splatters. In steady, gentle rain it is possible to close one's eyes and hear an entire landscape, its variable surface textures picked out in the pattern of sound.[2] But as rain turns to snow, the landscape vanishes from hearing. It is as though someone has switched off the sound. True, the first snow of winter can rattle like rain, especially if it is close to sleet in its consistency. Hitting the ground, it melts immediately, if it has not already melted. But as the ground itself freezes, the melting ceases. The flake, touching down on the cold bare surface, lies where it fell, its featherweight form intact, quivering in expectation. At any moment it could be picked up by the breeze and carried somewhere else, to one of those sheltered corners – such as a doorway or the lee of a tree-stump – where flakes tend to congregate.

Every snowflake is different. Although the basic hexagonal geometry is constant, the flake forms as it falls, and no two trajectories are exactly alike. In its precise form, the flake tells a story of its journey to earth. Much can happen along the way: it may grow through accretion, melt and refreeze, or stick to other flakes to form large multi-crystal assemblages that look like splodges in the sky. In a still wind, you can follow them by eye. Their course, sensitive to the slightest stirring of the air, is slow and erratic, often rising as well as falling, bounced this way and that by invisible currents. Unlike raindrops – which fall so fast there's no making them out unless or until they land obliquely, as on a window pane – flakes don't want to land. The wind, sweeping the surface of the earth, carries the flakes with it, so that when they do eventually land, they don't beat on the ground but come down gliding, at an acute angle. As more flakes fall, each alights almost noiselessly on others like itself, nestling among its predecessors. Gradually, imperceptibly, a white mantle forms over the earth. And as it does so, the earth – it seems – falls into a deep sleep. All sound is muffled. The silence is deafening. Only the wind sighs as it shakes the trees or blows the lying snow into drifts.

Usually, so long as snow is falling, the air is not especially cold, although it may chill you to the marrow if the wind gets up. This is because it is the mixing of cold with warmer air that leads to precipitation. It is when the snow eases off, the skies clear and the wind drops that the real cold sets in. Bone dry and at high pressure, the air lies heavily on frost-bitten earth. From the chimneys of houses and factories, smoke rises vertically skywards. Once again, the silence is overwhelming. But this is not a muffled silence, as when fresh snow is falling. Quite to the contrary: it seems as if the slightest sound – of ice cracking, of twigs snapping, of a barking dog or human voice – can travel for miles, punctuating the silence like a pin prick. There is a physical explanation for this, for sound travels faster in warm air than in cold. When warmer air is above and colder air below, sound waves are refracted downwards, thus bringing the most distant sounds to our ears. We hear them as a scattering of points, not unlike the way we see stars in the night sky.

That is, until the wind gets up, and prickly silence gives way to all-consuming tumult. Snow, whipped up from where it lay, is on the move again, cast into drifts. The Scots dialect compares this upward-rising drift of snow to its coming down as *erd-drift* (or *yowden-drift*) to *doon-come*.[3] In the whiteout of a snowstorm, earth and sky are indistinguishable, and the traveller is cast amidst a groundless void with no horizon. But wind unaided produces no sound. There must be something to funnel, interrupt or deflect the movement of air, to set it in vibration. Those of us who live in cities often associate the howling gales of winter with the moaning sounds produced as the wind plays on overhead wires and rooftop aerials, or as it squeezes through the cracks and crevices of buildings. But in forests, marshes and mountains, far from human habitation, different sounds are heard. Trees act like woodwind instruments, swamps like snare drums, mountains like brass. The wind, as it blows, is the player. It sings through trees like a flute, rattles the reed-beds of the frozen marshes like a drum, blasts through mountain gullies like a trombone.

It is the wind that carries the snow through its first life, its life in the air as budding flakes. On settling, however, snow enters a second life, its life on the ground as an ever-thickening mantle. This life can last for hours, days, months, seasons, years, centuries or even millennia. Under the mantle may be buried the evidence of past ages, only now coming back to light as the world warms and the melt accelerates. Inside, flakes congeal into an icy mass, peppered with air bubbles and particles of dirt, of a consistency that nevertheless changes continuously, depending – among other things – on ambient temperature, heat exchanges in the earth on which it lies, and compression from further falls. The reflecting properties of the surface change as well, yielding to many moods, if not shades, of white, from dull and brooding to light and sparkling. And so do its sounds, from the almost inaudible snap, crackle and pop of freezing ice and bursting bubbles to the roar of the avalanche or, on a lesser scale, the thud of snow falling from a sloping roof.

Animals whose lives are bound up with snow-cover recognize its sounds, above all, in the ways it rubs up against their own activity – often in digging, scraping and pawing to reach sources of food below. Cycles of thawing and refreezing, which turn the crust iron-hard, can spell hunger or even starvation. For those that can, a wiser option is to hibernate. Sleeping it out, they hear nothing until woken by the sounds of spring. But for human beings, the sound of lying snow is mostly heard underfoot, when travelling. Frosty snow squeaks when you tread on it, as its tiny crystalline plates slide against one another. Wet snow crunches as it is compressed, leaving deep prints which, being the last to melt, stand clear of the ground surface when the rest is gone. A hard crust grates under skis or sledge-runners. Today, however, the loudest sounds are likely to come from the drone of snowmobile engines, drowning out all else. From a distance these roaring machines sound, and look, more like gnats, buzzing out of season.

The sounds of snow are echoed in our spoken words. In almost every language, weather-words are infused with a rich strain of onomatopoeia, and words for snow are no exception. You would not have to be a speaker of Scots, for example, to fathom the meaning of *glushie* ('slush') or of Finnish to guess which of the two words, *lumi* and *räntä*, is for sleet and which for snow. As with the English words, so also in Finnish, hard consonants contrast with soft, and acute vowels with rounded ones. They conjure up the difference between rattling drops of sleet and softly whispering snowflakes. There is, however, a difference between the two languages which is of more far-reaching significance. In English, the word *snow* already incorporates the idea of its falling from the sky, as does *rain*. Water, or moisture, can be rain *only* in its falling; ergo water that stands, runs or lies, whether above or under the ground, cannot be rain. But in Finnish, the idea of falling is strictly separate from *what* falls. There is just one verb, *sataa*, for 'to fall from the sky', and anything that falls from the sky is *sade*.

The verb itself, along with its reflexive counterpart, *sattua* ('to befall'), is ancient, its origins lost in the mists of time. From the former is derived the word for harvest, *sato*; from the latter the word for a tale or story, *satu*. The harvest is a fall of grain, albeit not actually from the sky, but nevertheless thanks to the weather and by grace of the heavenly fortune that ordained it. The tale is a chronicle of things befallen, of happenings. It cannot, then, literally rain or snow in Finnish, but both water and snow can happen to fall. The verb *sataa* must always be followed by a specification of what, exactly, is falling, whether it be water, snow, sleet, hail, grain or metaphorical cats and dogs. Thus while rain is *vesisade* and snow is *lumisade*, neither the word for water (*vesi*) nor the word for snow (*lumi*) contains any hint of its descent from the sky. The primary condition of snow is to lie, just as water's primary condition is to run.

In a country like Finland, snow – like water – belongs first and foremost to the earth, not to the sky. This is no wonder, perhaps, in a country studded with lakes and in which it is usual for snow to lie for between four and six months of the year. But in springtime, when the snow sinks and melts, collapsing into itself like a sodden blanket, the land is suddenly awash, with rivers bursting their banks and fields often flooded. Water runs all over the place. As everywhere across the far North, however, weather patterns are shifting. The seasons are less sharply demarcated than before. Midwinter rainfall and midsummer snowfall are no longer exceptional. Birds and insects come and go at irregular times. The idea that the winters of the future might echo to the sounds of rain and running water, and that summers might lose the sounds of birds and insects, is deeply unnerving. The sky, it seems, is playing havoc with the earth. In Finnish they say, *semmosta sattuu* – 'that's what happens'. It's what comes down to us, or *doon-come*, as the Scots would pronounce it. Noisy winters and silent summers: we may just have to get used to them.

GOING TO GROUND

Introduction

What is the best way to become invisible, to disappear? If you were a criminal, a spy, a magician or even a wildlife photographer, this could be a matter of some practical consequence. You are advised to cover your tracks, to lie low, to go to ground. Whatever you do, avoid standing out! But you remain perplexed. What does it mean, you inquire, to cover things, to aim low rather than stand high, to inhabit the ground? Answers are not easy to come by, but in the following essays I shall try out a few possibilities. Here, by way of introduction, I set out three key terms around which these experiments revolve: cover, lowness and ground.

One way to hide is to adopt a disguise, such as a mask to cover your face or a cloak to dress your body. The mask or cloak covers up, but the real you remains behind. What is covered up can also be uncovered. But what, then, of your face, or your body? Does it not have a covering of skin? Unless we regard the skin, too, as a disguise, masking an interior self, then we have to allow that a cover can reveal as well as conceal. A face can wear an expression as well as a mask, a body its travails as well as a cloak. One sort of cover can be stripped off, the other can only be wiped clean or erased. An undercover operator can use the ambiguity itself as a means to deceive, presenting one kind of cover as though it were the other. This is the trick of camouflage.

But the ground, too, can deceive. What appears to people in high places as a solid platform on which to build can open up to the lowly, human or non-human, into an entire milieu of habitation – a ground not for building, but in which to dwell. Height and depth register differently here: not as a third dimension, as unknown to ground-dwelling creatures as to the Flatlanders immortalized by Edwin Abbott in his classic fable,[1] whose world was confined to the two dimensions of a geometric plane, but as the experience of rising and falling. Nestling into the folds of the ground, you feel it buoying up your body until – as in a dream – it seems to give way beneath, and you find yourself tumbling into the abyss, to be saved in the nick of time on waking. Lying low means creeping lightly and cautiously, for only the thinnest of membranes separates life and death.

What, then, *is* the ground? A base on which everything is supported? A place of life and habitation? Or a threshold between the worlds of the living and the dead? It could be any or all of these things. Our ideas of time, memory and forgetting, however, depend on what we take the ground to be. Suppose it is renewed by turning, as by the plough of the husbandman. Then time will also cycle. The past comes up as the present goes down. What lies buried will never be forgotten until it has risen to the surface and is wiped clean. But if the ground is not turned but added to, layer upon layer, then time will register as a linear sequence. With every additional layer, its predecessors sink deeper into the past. They will never come up again. Can a buried past, then, sink so deep that it is disappeared forever, as forgotten as if it had never been? This is the question posed by the present, but only the future can answer it.

Scissors paper stone

What on earth is the ground? It is a surface, says the dictionary, upon which things or persons stand or move. But this leaves many questions unanswered. What kind of surface is this? Does it have one side or two? Does it cover the earth or cover it up? What lies above, and what beneath? As these questions mount up, the ground surface – which we so often take for granted as the foundation for everything else – becomes ever more of a puzzle. How might we begin to solve it?

The idea for this essay came during a journey from my home city of Aberdeen to Utrecht, in the Netherlands, in January 2019. I was on my way to speak at a seminar on the theme of 'Memory Studies and Materiality'. I had promised to reflect on how memories are written into the ground, and was searching for inspiration. As you will see, it came from an unlikely quarter. The essay is based on my presentation to the seminar.

I

Wherever there is ground, three things must be present: first, earth; second, air or atmosphere; and, third, beings living, growing and moving around. The ground, then, is a coming together of these three things: earth, atmosphere and inhabitants. The question of the ground evidently turns on how they act upon, or suffer under, one another. Thinking this through, I recalled an ancient children's game. Originating in China, it is at least two thousand years old, but is now so widespread that I am sure it will be familiar to readers everywhere. The game is called 'scissors paper stone'.

Two players, seated or standing face-to-face, simultaneously put out a hand in one of three possible shapes. The first, with index and middle fingers extended to form a V-sign, means scissors. The second, with a flat palm and outstretched fingers, means paper. And the third, a clenched fist, means stone. If both players put out the same shape, the round is drawn, but otherwise the rule is that scissors defeat paper, paper defeats stone, and stone defeats scissors. The beauty of the game lies in the fact that not one of its characters is all-powerful. Scissors can cut paper but are blunted by stone; paper can wrap stone but is cut by scissors; stone can blunt scissors but is wrapped by paper. Each can be both doer and what is done to – it can be the one that acts, or the one that suffers. Agency and sufferance are wrapped up in the cycle.

Could it be the same with the three things that come together to make up the ground? Suppose that we substitute inhabitants for scissors, earth for paper and atmosphere for stone. What happens? First, *inhabitants*, as they move around or grow, inscribe marks or paths or weave trails into the fabric of the earth. Second, *the earth*, wracked by massive geomorphological forces, erupts into bends, buckles, folds and cracks. And, third, *the atmosphere* with its weather – its winds, storms and rainfall – erodes the surface of the earth, wiping out the tracks and trails of its inhabitants. Or in short: inhabitants trump the earth, in the course of *inscription*; the earth trumps the atmosphere, in episodes of *eruption*; and the atmosphere trumps the lines of inhabitants, in processes of *erosion*. Thus, in place of cutting, wrapping and blunting in the game of scissors paper stone, we have a cycle of inscription, eruption and erosion. Each is different, none is all-powerful, but all partake in the ongoing formation of the ground. Let's consider each in turn.

Inscription goes along. The line 'goes out for a walk', as the artist Paul Klee famously described his practice of drawing, 'for the sake of the walk'.[1] Try drawing a line freehand on a sheet of paper. You will find that the movement of the hand that holds the pencil is already underway by the time the pencil-point alights onto the paper surface, and carries on after it has left. What remains on the surface is the trace of a movement. Though the trace continues only for so long as the point is in contact with the paper, the movement itself is without beginning or end. Such are the trails of inhabitants. Like life and time, they simply keep on going.

Eruption is equivalent to what happens if you take the sheet of paper on which you have drawn your line and slide it in at the same time from both sides so that it folds upwards. Were the surface of a more rigid or brittle material, it might form a crease, or eventually fracture along the line of a crack. Folds, cracks and creases are interruptions of the surface caused by stresses and strains intrinsic to the base material itself. Not only do they pay no respect to any lines already inscribed; they are also rendered simultaneously along their entire length. If any evidence were needed of this, we only have to consider the cracks and fault-lines caused by major earthquakes.

Erosion is quite unlike both inscription and eruption. Returning to your paper with its pencil-line, take up an eraser and try to rub it out. This calls for a back-and-forth, oscillatory gesture best described as a 'wipe'. Compared to inscription, where all the movement is drawn to a focus at the point, with wiping it is distributed over the surface. The wipe always overflows any delineations it seeks to erase. So likewise wind and rain, scouring and washing the earth, wipe the tracks and trails of inhabitants. 'Tracks do not last,' writes Tom Brown, an Apache-trained tracker from New Jersey. 'They fade, and as they dry, the wind sweeps them relentlessly level to ease its way across the ground.'[2]

II

Let's now put these three movements together. I start with inscription and erosion, before proceeding to eruption. Once again, the fate of lines on a page gives us a good analogy for what happens with inscriptions in the earth. This time, however, the example comes not from drawing with pencil on paper but from the medieval practice of writing with pen on parchment. As a writing material, parchment is highly absorbent. The ink sinks in. Compared with the mass-produced paper of today, moreover, parchment was rather expensive. For this reason, it was common for the same piece to be reused, over and over again. To do this, the surface would be scraped with a knife – the same knife that was used to sharpen the quill and score the guidelines – until the traces of previous writing had been erased. It was impossible, however, to remove them altogether. Thus vestiges of earlier inscriptions always remained. Rewriting on parchment bearing the partially erased inscriptions of preceding use results in what palaeographers call a *palimpsest*.

The remarkable thing about the palimpsest is that it is formed not by adding layer upon layer, each with its own inscriptions, but by taking them away. As a result, older traces rise up to the surface, even as newer ones sink down. We can best see how this occurs by means of a diagram (Figure 10). This shows a parchment in exaggerated cross-section, such that a line of ink appears as a vertical mark, as wide as the line is thick and as deep as the ink sinks into the fabric of the parchment. In the diagram I have indicated two lines inscribed at time T_0. Later, at time T_1, the surface is scraped, and two new lines are inscribed close to the old ones. The same is done again at time T_2. Now, looking at the surface at T_2, observe what has happened to the traces. The original traces from T_0 are only just visible right at the surface, and will surely disappear if the parchment is used again. The

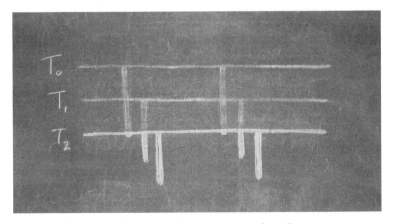

Figure 10 Exaggerated cross-section of a palimpsest.
(Photo by the author.)

traces from T_1 are shallower than they were, but still clear. Deepest of all are the most recent traces, from T_2.

Archaeologists and landscape historians have adopted the concept of the palimpsest to refer to a ground that, over the ages, has been repeatedly used, eroded and used again. Just like the earliest inscriptions on parchment, the most ancient tracks, worn by feet from centuries past, are now barely visible traces on the surface, on the point of vanishing. It may take a specialist eye to see them. Unless artificially preserved, the weather will soon wipe them out altogether. By contrast, the newest incisions, recently cut in the landscape and not yet subject to significant erosion, are strongly marked. In between are historic traces that, while manifestly weather-beaten and sometimes obscured, are still easy to recognize. Thus in the land as on parchment, the past is not buried under the present but actually closest to the surface, while the present, undercutting the past, digs deepest. The past rises, even as the present descends. This is not a layering so much as a *turning over*. I shall return to this idea of the turnover. First, however, we need to complete the picture by reintroducing the movement of eruption.

III

This is to focus not on lines in the earth but on the earth itself, as it rises up to meet the sky. Throughout geological time, the dialogue of earth and atmosphere has always pitted the former's force of eruption against the latter's force of erosion. Between the two – between earth and atmosphere – lies the ground. But this ground is not an interface. An interface, by definition, is a surface of measurable thickness that separates what is on either side while at the same time affording channels of communication between one side and the other. In Figure 11, I have drawn how the ground would look, in cross-section, were it an interface. Bear in mind that the diagram is nothing if not schematic, and that the arcs of earth and atmosphere denote affective horizons rather than actual physical boundaries, of which, of course, there are none.

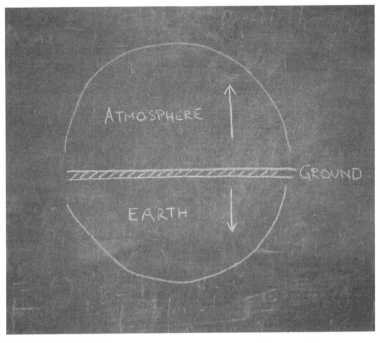

Figure 11 Earth, atmosphere and ground as interface.
(Photo by the author.)

In reality, however, the ground has no topside or underside. It doesn't hold earth and atmosphere apart. On the contrary, it is the zone of their interpenetration. It is where the earth with its materials and the atmosphere with its weather meet and carry on their eternal conversation. It is where rain meets soil and turns it to mud, where wind meets sand and blows it into dunes, where snow meets ice and coats the surface in a blanket of white. The earth's eruption thrusts the ground up from below; atmospheric erosion grinds it down from above. The ground surface, however, has depth but no thickness. Should we attempt to measure it, we would find that starting from the lower, atmospheric horizon, there is no limit to how far up we could go and that, conversely, starting from the upper, earthly one, we could keep on going down without ever reaching rock bottom. Figure 12 shows – again schematically and in cross-section – what this would look like.

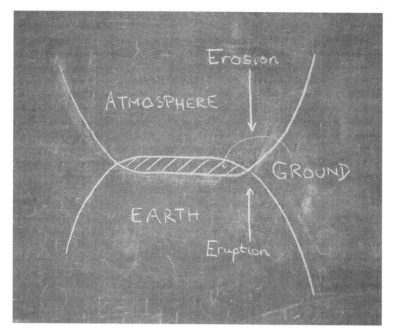

Figure 12 The ground at the meeting of earth and atmosphere.
(Photo by the author.)

Observing a landscape of meadows and forests, moors and mountains, John Ruskin – Victorian art critic and social thinker extraordinaire – thought he saw the earth covered by a 'veil of strange intermediate being'.[3] Deep down, Ruskin argued, the earth is dead and cold, but at its surface it ministers to its inhabitants through this veil: 'which breathes, but has no voice; moves, but cannot leave its appointed place; passes through life without consciousness . . .'. It is a veil that covers but doesn't cover *up*, an in-between that can be inhabited but not crossed. Rise up, and the veil also lifts; sink down, and it falls. So it is with the ground: rise or fall, there is no going through.

IV

With this, we can finally revert to the idea of the turnover, and to the game of scissors paper stone from which I began. We have seen how inhabitants cut their lines into the earth as scissors cut paper; how the rising earth swells into the atmosphere, veiling it as paper wraps stone; and how atmospheric weather grinds down the lines of inhabitants as stone blunts scissors. Together they constitute a cycle that has ever turned with the passage of time. The ground is formed in the cycle. It exists only in the turnover: in the movements of inscription, eruption and erosion as they bear upon one another. It is equivalent to neither scissors, nor paper, nor stone. It is equal, rather, to the game itself.

What does all this mean for the way we think about memory? Our modern sensibilities are profoundly conditioned by the idea that everything is formed of layers – that the ground, trees, buildings, books and even human minds are built up, layer upon layer, with each layer already marked up with its own notations, whether numerical, graphic or diagrammatic. The past, then, is visible only by way of the translucence of the present. But the logic of the palimpsest teaches us otherwise. It tells us that with the passage of time, layers are not added but worn away, and that to mark them up means cutting deep. As in the palimpsest, our oldest memories are not the deepest, nor are the most recent the shallowest. On the contrary, what is furthest in the past is closest to the surface. In our minds as well as in the ground we tread, our recent deeds and words are most profoundly seared, while traces of the distant past are so shallow as to be on the point of disappearing altogether, erased by the winds of present suffering. Like old paths grown so faint as to be no longer recognizable, memories only truly fade as they rise to the surface; prior forgetfulness is mere inadvertence.

There is a lesson here for tyrants everywhere, who believe that their murderous acts can be forgotten by burying them underground. They imagine the ground as a cover-up, thinking that beneath it, the evidence can be forever concealed from posterity. This is literally to overlook the past, in both senses – of surveillance and neglect. But buried deeds have their come-uppance, and will only be forgotten for good when they finally surface, to be wiped clean by the ravages of time.

Ad coelum

This piece began with a request from the anthropologist Franck Billé to contribute to a collection of short essays on the topic of 'volumetric sovereignty'.[1] *The core argument behind the collection was that recent technological developments have made it possible for nation-states to assert control over, and attempt to colonize, previously inaccessible realms both above and below the earth's surface. The reach of sovereign power upwards and downwards, at ever greater scales, seems to require us to reimagine the state as occupying a three-dimensional volume rather than a flat surface.*

I had not come across the concept of volumetric sovereignty before. Intrigued, and wondering how it reflected on changing understandings of the ground, I accepted the challenge. In the course of my inquiries, I made two discoveries which were new, at least to me. One was that only as the result of a long history has 'volume' come to mean the three-dimensional extent we take it for today. The other was the venerable legal principle of ad coelum. *Both are explained in what follows, which I have revised from the originally published version.*

Cuius est solum, eius est usque ad coelum et ad inferos.
Whoever's is the soil, it is theirs all the way to heaven and all the way to hell.

This principle of property law, commonly abbreviated as the *ad coelum* doctrine, is attributed to the thirteenth-century Italian jurist Accursius, and entered into the common law of England during the reign of Edward I (1272–1307). It means that, at least in theory, if I own a piece of ground, it is mine not just at the surface but upwards into the air, and downwards into the earth, as far as one can go. In modern times, the advent of air travel, on the one hand, and sub-surface mining and fracking operations, on the other, have severely tested the doctrine, putting limits on both the upward and downward extent of individual property rights. The ground has, as it were, been boxed in. Yet on a larger scale the principle still applies, since the individual's property-box is nested within a much larger box, namely that of the sovereign state. For the jurisdiction of the state, in modern times, is not just territorial but volumetric, including its claims both to air space and to underground resources, at heights and depths far beyond the limits of individual entitlement.

Statutory law, in short, has accorded volume to the ground, but only by adding a third dimension, of verticality, to the two dimensions of its putatively horizontal surface. However, there is a sense of much more ancient provenance, buried in agrarian custom and practice, in which the surface of the ground is *intrinsically* voluminous. To find this sense, you do not have to escape the surface, either upwards or downwards. You have, rather, to roll it up or turn it over. Indeed the word 'volume' has its source in these very operations. It comes from the Latin *volvere*, 'to roll'. Thus it is cognate with such words as 'evolution' and 'revolution'. The original volume was a scroll of papyrus or parchment, usually inscribed with writing. To read it, the scroll had to be unrolled, or *evolved*, after which it would be rolled up again, or *revolved*. Only later did the scroll give way to the handwritten codex, and eventually to the printed book. The result was to transform the meaning of volume from the roll to the size or extent in three dimensions by which we know it today.

In the codex, the continuous length of the scroll would be folded into sheets, like a concertina, so that the reader, rather than unrolling the volume, would turn its pages, opening up each fold only to close its predecessor behind. On turning the page, *recto* to *verso*, what had once been hidden would be revealed, and what had been open concealed. Although every sheet had two sides, there was no going through: you could only get from one side to the other by the simultaneous folding and unfolding of the turn. And the codex itself – never

Figure 13 Open codex and closed book in cross-section.
(Photo by the author.)

closed but always open, in the reader's hands or on their desk – lent itself to this. It would be seen, rather like a modern newspaper, not in its thickness but in the spread of its pages. Not until the manuscript was replaced by the printed word was the book finally closed. For in the printed book, the pages are laid one over another to form a stack. Although you still have to turn the pages to read it, the book itself is now perceived as a thing of layered sheets to be worked *through*, top to bottom as beginning to end.

Figure 13, showing the open codex and the closed book in diagrammatic cross-section, illustrates this difference between folding and stacking, and between turning the pages and reading through. Nowadays, when you retrieve what you call a 'volume' from your shelf, it is to the layered stack that you refer. Bound between covers, it takes on something of the character of a box. The volume has become a container, and the words its contents. By extension, then, the volume of any form, whether material like a wooden box or ideal like an abstract geometrical figure, becomes the measure of its capacity to contain. And with that, the voluminous makes way for the volumetric.

Now let's get back to ground. Can it be compared to a scroll? Can it be rolled up on itself, and unrolled, like a carpet? Roll up a carpet, and you will find that the underside lifts up over the topside, which now finds itself beneath. The ground cannot, of course, be rolled or unrolled quite like that. But it can be turned. Put yourself into the shoes of the medieval ploughman, who would turn the ground with every turn of the seasons in the agricultural calendar. There were three periods of ploughing in the medieval year: in April for spring crops, June for the late summer harvest and October for winter wheat and rye. The purpose of ploughing is to bring to the surface nutrient-rich soil from deep down, while burying soil already drained of nutrients by previous cropping, along with any remaining weeds and stubble. Thanks to this recurrent turnover, the ground will continue to yield, year after year. It is repeatedly renewed, not by adding layer upon layer as in a stack, but by breaking it, cutting through with the share so as to raise the deep and bury the shallow.

That's what makes the ground surface – like the carpet and the codex – into a volume. It's a surface that turns with the seasonal passage of time, with the alternations of weather and the husbandry of crops, wherein the past rises up even as the present sinks below. This is a ground not just of cultivation but of memory. For with its turning, memories of persons who lived or events that happened long ago are brought to the surface so that inhabitants can engage with them directly, as if present in the here and now. This is how books were read in medieval times, as aids to living memory. They were read aloud, while fingers traced the letters. It was as if the pages spoke with the voices of the past, brought back to life. So, likewise, would the ground speak to the husbandman, with the bounty of previous harvests. Seeds, planted in the soil as words on the page, would spring to life in their germination and growth. Following a cycle of rotation, a fertility born of the past would bear fruit in the present, reviving memories with the flourishing of each season's crops.

But with the volume reconceived as a box or container, with contents layered in a stack, time no longer rolls, folds or turns the ground. It rather pierces through successive grounds like an arrow, pointing either upwards from past to present, or downwards from present to past. Here every ground, every layer, establishes its own plane of synchrony, while layer succeeds layer in a diachronic sequence. To reach the past, as in archaeological excavation, you have to dig down. Memory here is like an archive, deposited in stacks with the oldest records furthest down. There they stay, sinking ever deeper as time moves on. As a deposit, the past contains no potential for renewal. It is over. Renewal can come only from superimposition, by adding another layer to the stack, then another, and then yet another. Each successive layer is understood to be a fundamental platform – level, void and hard – upon which everything stands, each in its proper location, as might be represented on a cartographic map. This is the ground as territory, conceived within the apparatus of the state.

In the eyes of the state, the ground is not for turning. It is for occupation. The logic is territorial. The state does not inscribe its ways into the land as does the husbandman, or like the penman into parchment, but rather imposes its sovereignty from above, much as, with the printing press, letters are imposed upon the sheet. Every new impression, then, calls for a new sheet, or a new ground. Yet the ground itself, were it conceived only as territory, would have no volume, only area. How, then, can a state whose territory is confined to the ground of the present simultaneously establish sovereignty over volume? It can do so only by setting aside the ground surface for spaces above and below, respectively aerial and subterranean. To the two dimensions of the horizontal it is necessary to add a third, of height above or depth below the zero point. All movement, then, is plotted on an abstract grid of three dimensions. One can go across, from place to place in the territory, but also vertically up and down, as in an elevator.

That's why for architects aiming to pierce the sky with their constructions, air transport engineers looking to build a runway or space scientists who would send rockets to the moon, the ground is not a surface to be turned but a level plane – a ground zero – from which to ascend. Like a foundation, runway or launch-pad, it should be flat, hard-surfaced and free from obstruction. Conversely, for prospectors seeking to bore for oil or gas, or minerals, or for physicists who would go to great depths to conduct their experiments on the fundamental properties of matter, the ground is a plane from which to drill down. What were the realms of heaven and hell, respectively divine and diabolical, for the originators of the *ad coelum* doctrine are now divided into the volumetric compartments of a utopian space. Whether aerial or subterranean, such space can be surveyed and apportioned but cannot truly be inhabited. Empty and featureless, it has no place for life to take root and grow. Nevertheless in today's world, it is in the reckoning of space, and not the revolution of time, that volume is produced.

Are we afloat?

The Musée des arts et métiers, *founded in Paris in 1794 for the preservation and display of scientific instruments and inventions, is housed in what had once been the medieval priory of Saint-Martin-des-Champs. It is a place full of legends, one of which tells of a spring or stream which could once have supplied the monks with their water and might even have been the reason why the priory was originally sited where it was. Even today, on occasion, water has been observed to seep through the flagstones in the chapel tower, a part of the building not normally open to visitors.*

In 2019, artist Anaïs Tondeur and anthropologist Germain Meulemans chose this site as the setting for a remarkable installation, entitled Paris flotte-t-il? *('Is Paris Floating?').*[1] *Hovering on the borders between fact and fiction, the installation recreates in light and sound the miraculous journey of a diviner who has allegedly slipped into the tower to solve, once and for all, the mystery of where the water is coming from. Lifting a flagstone, he is suddenly engulfed as the earth gives way beneath him. Falling through the void, he finds himself in a labyrinth of pipes, tunnels and streams, leading eventually to a cavernous, dreamy world, both darkly menacing and eerily beautiful, in which everything is dripping, trickling and oozing. The earth itself has become liquid, and the buildings above appear to be either drifting like the hulls of ships in the ocean, or supported on piles driven down to bedrock. Seen from below, is the city really afloat?*

For visitors, the installation affords a kind of inverted periscope through which to peer into this aqueous subterranean world, as if down a well-shaft, and to join the diviner on his journey. They return with a new-found awareness of the contingent solidity of surfaces we routinely take for granted as we go about our lives above ground, and of the huge effort

*needed to engineer a built environment that, for its inhabitants, is secure
and dry. For myself, it caused me to reflect once again on the meaning of
the ground, and it led to the following essay, which was commissioned
and published (in French) in a booklet to accompany the installation. I
have revised and expanded the essay for this volume.*

A small area of my garden is paved with flagstones. I wonder: do these
stones partake of the ground? I can stand on them, or walk over them,
and they offer pretty firm support. With effort, I could also lift them.
What, then, would I find beneath? Why, surely, another ground! This
time, however, it would be a ground of soil, maybe threaded with the
roots of the weeds that tend to grow between cracks in the pavement.
Maybe, too, I would discover a variety of creatures, from earwigs to
millipedes, whose place of shelter I have brutally exposed. The paving
stones that had once been *of* the ground, now lifted and stacked,
have become objects *on* it. But for the weeds, the ground was never
a surface to stand on to begin with; it was rather the very milieu or
matrix of their growth and formation. As for the earwigs and the
millipedes, for them the ground is less a surface of habitation than a
medium. They are used to living and moving *in* it, not *upon* it. It offers
the means of passage, rather than a foundation of support. If you were
a millipede, you would use your legs for burrowing, not for standing!

The paved surface, hard and unyielding, closes off the earth below
from contact with the air above. It has a topside and an underside.
For life to flourish, there must be gaps or fissures that allow a passage
between the two. The weeds, millipedes and earwigs are denizens of
the cracks. In the soft and squishy ground of soil, by contrast, the
earth opens to the atmosphere – to its light and shade, its turbulence,
and its variations of heat and humidity. This opening ground is where
the earth rises to embrace the sky, its temperate surface continuously
formed by the mixing and blending of the two. But by the same token,
the opening ground, the earth's rising, has no underside. It covers
nothing but itself. A hole in the open ground is a pit, not an orifice; to
break such ground – as with the ploughshare – is to engrave the earth,

to mark it with striations, but not to cut it into strips. You can fall *into* open ground, into its pits and troughs, but you cannot fall *through* it. You can make footprints in soft, open ground, but on the closed, hard pavement you can only stamp, leaving no mark save that left by the dirt on the soles of your shoes.

Reflecting on pavement and soil, I wonder whether all ground is caught in a double movement, of opening up and closing off, of exposure and encrustation. To stand or even fall on opening ground is to be held in its embrace, and to feel its immeasurable depth. The support it offers is unconditional. But the depth of closing ground is not felt at the surface. It is a measured depth, given in the thickness of its crust, between topside and underside. Moreover, it offers only conditional support, dependent on the carrying capacity of its constituent materials. Like ice, it could give way if too thin to bear the weight placed on it. But precisely because it is double, the ground can deceive. Unsuspecting inhabitants may roam the open, confident of earthly support while insensible to the cavernous voids beneath, until the sudden appearance of a sinkhole catches them out and they are dropped, like the diviner of Saint-Martin-des-Champs, into a nether world of whose existence they had been completely unaware. This underworld, too, has its ground, where the lower earth rises to meet its own atmosphere. Yet what is atmosphere for the inhabitants of such a world would be earth for us; what allows them to move and breathe would, in our world, presage immobility, suffocation and even death.

Indeed, even as we go about our business, safe in the conviction that, whatever happens, the ground offers a secure foundation on which to build our lives, we are nevertheless stalked by the spectre of mortality – by the fear that the ground is but the thinnest of crusts, suspended between life and death, above and below, this world and the underworld. The very ground that, in life, opens up to embrace its inhabitants, in death closes over them. In this double movement, of opening and closure, lies the peculiarly human art of burial. When burying a body, we first open up the earth and lay the body in its midst; then we close it over with a slab. Where initially it was laid *in* the ground, it is finally entombed *below* the ground. In time, vegetation will grow over the site, contributing to the formation of a layer of soil, eventually leaving the grave indistinguishable from its surroundings, save perhaps for a small hump or a stone to mark its location. The burial chamber remains hidden, until such time as it is broken through by surface excavations, not just because it is obscured from prying eyes, but because, at the surface, the earth again appears to rise to meet the sky. Everything looks and feels open to the elements; there is no hint of a cover-up.

And yet we are deceived, by a forgetfulness born of neglect and inadvertence rather than genuine loss. A buried past can never truly be forgotten, but it can be falsely so. A past truly forgotten is brought to the surface only to fade into nothingness, but to forget a buried past is to fall for the illusion the ground plays on us – to mistake the closing ground, with its topside and underside, for an opening ground with neither. There have been plenty of efforts, in both fact and fiction, to collude in the deception. In the climax of the James Bond film *You Only Live Twice*, what appears to be a natural lake in a volcanic crater turns out to be a sliding metal roof concealing a massive, cavernous operation to send a rocket into space. On a less spectacular scale, but this time in fact, planners for the city of Aberdeen recently proposed an urban garden in the city centre, complete with lawns, fountains and trees, that would roof over a major road, railway line and car park. Publicity for the scheme, which was never realized, pictured happy, leisured citizens aimlessly wandering about in this pastoral landscape, oblivious to the engines of transport grinding away beneath and filling the stagnant air with their exhaust.

In several countries today, plans are afoot to bury the radioactive wastes of nuclear technologies deep in disused mineshafts, where they can be left to decay over the millennia, unknown to the inhabitants of a ground projected to revert to pristine woodland and to provide a haven for wildlife. Those on the surface, inhabiting the ground and breathing the air of the open, would have no idea of the poison insidiously percolating from below. No records would remain, no secrets for future investigation to uncover. But if today's technocrats are willing to perpetrate such monstrous deception on generations to come, then what tricks might already have been played on us by generations past, of which we know nothing? Will the depositions of the present ever be as forgotten as ancient cities are today, now buried under desert sands? Are we destined to live our lives on the opening ground betwixt earth and sky, oblivious to what lies beneath, or are we rather fated to drift on the glass ceiling of a nether world wherein, as in the bowels of the *Musée des arts et métiers*, the souls of the dead mingle with the relics and residues of human industry? Are we grounded or afloat? Our lot, it seems, is to oscillate between the two.

Shelter

Frustrated by soaring property prices and escalating homelessness in London, the artist Tim Knowles hit on the idea of researching possibilities for finding shelter in the very different surroundings of the Scottish Highlands. Could this apparently inhospitable environment offer clues to another way of dwelling? The region had suffered historically from depopulation, caused by the wholesale eviction of tenant farmers, leaving many abandoned buildings, most now in ruins. Today the right to roam, promoting access to land for recreation and exercise, sits uneasily with the continued enclosure of large areas within private estates managed for grouse shooting and owned by absentee landlords. Looking to set up a network of hidden shelters in this landscape, Knowles had not only to contend with the elements but also to operate under the noses of potentially aggressive gamekeepers. In Scots, the shelter is a howff, *literally a haunt, a place into which a body can pass unnoticed while yet infusing the milieu with its presence. In Knowles's project, every* howff *was a minimally obtrusive sculptural intervention in the landscape, with a location known only to himself. He would share his experiences, however, in a publication to accompany the project, and I was asked to contribute to it.[1] The result was this essay, on the theme of 'shelter'.*

Shelter, we suppose, is a fundamental human need. But this raises many questions. Is it a need particular to humans, or shared by animals of other kinds? What, exactly, do we shelter from? And by what means? For many, no doubt, the first thing that comes to mind in thinking of shelter is the weather. We shelter from pouring rain while waiting for a bus, from biting wind while huddling behind a wall, from cold while warming ourselves before the fire in a lean-to, or from the sun while reclining under a parasol on the beach. Human beings are not well equipped by nature to withstand wind and rain, snow and freezing temperatures, or the glare and extreme heat of the sun. We catch cold easily, and are equally prone to heatstroke. Storm, flood and drought can place lives in peril – and not only human lives, for they can equally imperil the lives of the many domestic animals that have grown accustomed to their human guardians for protection. To non-human animals living beyond the ambit of human protection, however, the weather does not generally pose such a hazard. By and large, they are well adapted to withstand it. The principal danger, for them, comes not from meteorological forces but from other creatures. Prey, not predators, have greatest need of shelter. If you are a small animal, you could retreat into a crevice or burrow, beyond the reach of your larger attacker. Or you could adopt a camouflage, hiding in plain sight by remaining perfectly immobile and indistinguishable from your surroundings. Neither option, however, is realistic for larger animals, such as herds of ungulates, which tend to find safety in numbers and, in the last resort, in a capacity for rapid flight. Humans, being of moderate build and relatively slow afoot, can rarely outrun a predator, nor can they easily fit into cracks that predators cannot reach. Their trump card, however, lies in an unusual ability to configure things differently from how they are, or to rearrange what is to hand in ways that answer to their predicament. It can usually be relied upon to get them out of a tight spot.

In bygone times, large predators such as bears, wolves and tigers presented a significant danger to humans. Nowadays these animals are mostly confined to remote and sparsely populated regions, and are no longer the threat they once were. Far greater has always been the threat from fellow humans. Indeed there is some evidence that the word 'shelter' comes from the Old English word for 'shield', and more specifically the battle formation of many shields locked together to form a kind of wall. Over time, shelters have evolved along with offensive techniques for overwhelming them. The solid walls of medieval fortresses thickened to withstand the barrage of cannon-shot, while in the course of the past century, people in many parts of the world have been forced to take shelter from aerial bombardment. From air-raid shelters and subterranean tunnels to nuclear bunkers, the pyrotechnic threat from the skies, delivered by their own kind, has driven otherwise defenceless humans ever deeper underground, beyond the reach of natural light and fresh air. In times of war, where death and destruction visit the surface of the earth, the living have to find shelter in places of burial beneath it, insensible to the mayhem going on above.

However, there is another way to find shelter – from offensive operations, if not necessarily from the weather – than by digging down or building defensive structures. This is to contrive a *hide*. The hide works on the opposite principle to the fortress. It is not a structure of resistance, engineered to withstand an onslaught directed from without, but a flimsy assemblage that turns to account whatever may be afforded by features of the environment that are already there, or – if anything is to be constructed at all – using lightweight materials immediately to hand. It is because these materials are virtually indistinguishable from those around and about, and because of the minimal modification of landscape features, that the hide is so hard to spot. And it is this invisibility that offers inhabitants their best protection. As we say colloquially, they 'go to ground'. The ground provides places of hiding or shelter for its inhabitants precisely because it is not a solid and featureless platform upon which all else rests, but an intricately folded or crumpled volume of heterogeneous materials. To go to ground, then, is to nestle into a fold much as you would into a cradle, co-opting its existing features with only the barest of additions. It could be a crevice or an overhang in the rock, a nook in the canopy of a tree or a hollow in the earth (Figure 14). In order to access the cradle and snuggle in, however, the inhabitant may have to climb, twist or crawl, executing movements that demand of the body a flexibility to which it grows unaccustomed with advancing years.

Besides going to ground, however, an alternative or additional way to hide is to 'go under cover', adopting the ground not as a refuge but as a disguise. This is the trick of camouflage. It works by deceiving onlookers into taking one kind of surface for another. We are inclined

Figure 14 Shelter in a rocky overhang.
(Photo by Tim Knowles, courtesy of the artist.)

to think of the surface as a layer, covering up what lies beneath, and separating it from what lies above. But the ground is not naturally like that. Not only is it open to the sky; it is also of infinite depth. You can bore *into* it, but not *through* it. Above, it might be thick with vegetation, which we readily liken to a carpet. Yet we know that whereas a carpet can be lifted to reveal its underside, the ground cannot. It doesn't have an underside. It is a cover, not a cover-*up*. The trick of camouflage is to pretend that what is really a layered surface, with a topside and an underside like a carpet, is a deep surface like that of the earth, covering only itself. Thus the soldier, dressed in a costume whose mottled colours mimic those of his surroundings, his face plastered with mud, appears to vanish. Likewise the hunter can lie concealed within a hide made of leaves, sticks and branches indistinguishable from those that litter the forest floor.

The shelter, if you will, is an inverted trap. Both shelter and trap involve an element of subterfuge. The trap works by tempting the unsuspecting victim to enter into its fold, perhaps with the reward of a bait, only for a concealed door to snap shut. Or it tricks the unwary to tread on what looks like solid ground, only to fall through into a pit concealed below. Entering a shelter, you might likewise pass through a trapdoor or a hatch, which closes behind you, but in this case you are not fooled. For whereas the trap is set up by outside agencies, putting you at risk of falling in or being caught, with the shelter it is the other way around: you are the one who sets it up; you enter on purpose, while the deceit is practised on the authorities. Yet even in its innermost chambers, the shelter gives out to the open. It is a place-holder for life, but it is not a container. As a body must breathe in and out to live, the inhabitant must come and go. One cannot stay inside for long; residence is temporary. Shelter always alternates with exposure, within an open world of earth and sky.

That's why, relative to the interior spaces of modernity which aim to reconstruct within their walls a simulacrum of the open – an artificial, *as if* world already furnished with the conveniences of life – the shelter ever remains out of doors, even though one might have to pass through a hidden door, outwardly disguised as earth, in order to effect an entry (Figure 15). For the door or cover of the shelter stands on the threshold between earth and sky, not between the earth–sky world and its interior reconstruction. Finding shelter within the modern home is pretend play, as in the game of hide and seek, with furniture

Figure 15 Barrel shelter with door open.
(Photo by Tim Knowles, courtesy of the artist.)

standing in for rocky refuge and curtains for vegetative cover. Out in the open, however, hide and seek is for real. And whether achieved by going to ground or under cover, hiding means making the best of what an environment affords for protection. The inhabitant in search of shelter has therefore to be more alive than ever to the affordances of the environment. He or she may be solitary, but this solitude is anything but isolating, for it is grounded in a heightened perceptual attentiveness to the surroundings – an attentiveness that can extend to deep and sympathetic companionship towards others in a similar situation.

Such is the perception of the fugitive, the outlaw on the run from the authorities, and the poacher evading the notice of gamekeepers in the pay of unscrupulous landlords. They need their wits about them, to improvise with whatever is to hand, leaving little or no visible trace of their movements. We are inclined to romanticize such figures, to admire their bush-craft, to emulate their wit and ingenuity, and to celebrate the warmth of their fellowship. But that would be to turn a blind eye to the forces of oppression that, throughout history, have driven people from their homes, their lands and their countries. It has ever been the weak and vulnerable who have sought shelter, never the strong and powerful. The master does not seek shelter in his own house, but may offer it as charity to the destitute. Shelter implies dispossession on the part of those who seek it, and generosity on the part of its providers. Today the search for shelter speaks predominantly of homelessness, substance abuse, domestic breakdown, political and religious persecution and the vicissitudes of war. So when we declare that shelter is a universal human need, it is as well to remember that the universe of needs is structured by relations of power, and that neediness does not fall equally on all.

Doing time

I recently had the pleasure to meet the celebrated Taiwanese artist Tehching Hsieh. Hsieh's work had been the subject of an exhibition at the Taiwanese Pavilion in the 2017 Venice Biennale, and I had been invited to join a panel, including Hsieh himself, to reflect on it. While the work was new to me – I had never before come across Hsieh, or his art – its theme was not. It was about time and life, and the connection between them. But reflecting on the work led me to think about this theme in ways I had not previously considered. An invitation to contribute an article to LA+, an interdisciplinary journal of landscape architecture published by the School of Design at the University of Pennsylvania, in a themed issue on 'Time', afforded me an opportunity to commit these thoughts to paper.[1]

Tehching Hsieh's story is no ordinary one, as I found from my visit to the exhibition in Venice, as well as from my reading of a comprehensive volume on his life and work compiled by the writer and curator Adrian Heathfield, entitled *Out of Now.*[2] I learned how in 1967, as the seventeen-year-old son of a large middle-class family, with an authoritarian father and a doting mother, Hsieh had dropped out of high school and taken up painting; how in 1973, following army service and his first solo show, he abruptly stopped painting and made his first performance work by jumping out of a second-storey window onto the hard pavement below, breaking both his ankles and leaving him in constant pain for the rest of his life; how he went on to train as a seaman, as a means to work his way to the United States; how in 1974 he escaped down the gangplank of an oil-tanker moored on the Delaware River and made his way to Manhattan, where he eked out a living as an illegal immigrant, working in restaurants and construction sites until the thought came to him that the isolation and alienation he was experiencing could itself be a form of art. He would be the work.

What followed were six pieces, each remarkable for the tenacity with which it was pursued, and for its apparent futility. In the first, executed in 1978–9, Hsieh constructed a small cage of pine dowels in his New York loft, furnished only with a bed, sink and bucket, in which he lived for exactly a year, without company, without even acknowledging the presence of spectators who were occasionally permitted to watch, and without conversing, reading or writing. A friend brought food and emptied his bucket, but that was it. Every day he would scratch a line on the wall, and after 365 had elapsed he re-emerged. For the second piece, which followed in 1980–1 and again lasted precisely one year, Hsieh set himself the task of punching a factory time clock on the hour, every hour, twenty-four hours a day, every day of the year. With each punch of the clock, he shot a photographic frame of himself, standing erect, dressed in uniform (Figure 16). With only 133 missed calls, he ended up with 8,627 authenticated timecards and as many photographic frames, which, run rapidly in sequence on a cinematograph, comprise an extraordinary filmic record of the year.

Barely six months after completing this ordeal, Hsieh commenced a third one-year performance, in which he spent all of his time out of doors on the streets of New York City, refusing – according to his announcement of intent – to enter any 'building, subway, train, car, airplane, ship, cave, tent'. His only possession would be a sleeping bag. Every day he plotted his movements on a street map. The winter of 1981–2 was one of the coldest on record, during which the East River froze, and the privation was extreme. But only once was Hsieh forced to break his vow, when an altercation with a member of the public led to his arrest and detention for fifteen hours. Having completed this third ordeal, some nine months later Hsieh took up a fourth, this time conjointly with the artist Linda Montano. For one year, 1983–4, they were to live together without ever touching, while joined waist-to-waist by an eight-foot rope. The relationship, we

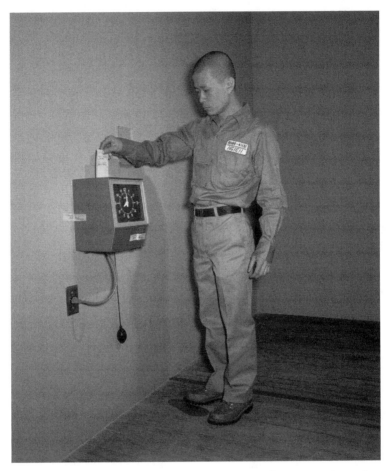

Figure 16 *Punching the Time Clock: One-Year Performance 1980–1981*, photo by Michael Shen. (© Tehching Hsieh, courtesy of Tehching Hsieh and Sean Kelly, New York. Reproduced with permission.)

learn, was not harmonious. It was, perhaps, mutually self-defeating. At any rate, it set the stage for piece number five, in which Hsieh was to abstain, again for a year, 1985–6, from having anything to do with art: he would not do it, talk about it, see it, read it, go to any gallery or visit any museum. 'I just go in life,' he announced. In a final act of renunciation, Hsieh cooked up his sixth piece, a 'thirteeen-year plan', starting on the last day of 1986 and ending at the turn of the millennium, during which he staged a complete disappearance. At the end of it he re-emerged to declare, simply, 'I kept myself alive.'

What kind of life was this? And why was Hsieh so obsessed with the passage of time?

Looking at the shots of Hsieh in his cage, posing by the clock, wandering the streets or tied to an unsympathetic companion, you would not get the impression of someone enjoying life. His expression is sullen and brooding, ranging from boredom to fatigue. Never do his eyes light up, nor is there any hint of a smile. Imagine my surprise, then, on meeting him for the first time – a man of my age, then in his late sixties – to be greeted by laughing eyes and a mischievous grin. It made me wonder: is there humour in this work? Does it raise the spirits? Could it be that what we see in the photographs is but the husk of a man who has found a kind of freedom that most of us dream of but never quite manage to attain? This, for me, became the question of the work. How can the self-imposition of a regime so constraining, so oppressive, so monotonous, so devoid of any possibility of progress, actually release the human spirit into the fullness of life?

For many, Hsieh's work is a lesson in self-obsessed pointlessness. A letter from an anonymous correspondent, dated April 1981, had this to say: 'We who utilize our education and intelligence to make the world a better place to live in are horrified by your stupidity and publicity for a crass self-display. Artist? Ugh!' Life, according to this correspondent – and doubtless to the majority who would think along the same lines – should be devoted to some productive purpose; it should be world-building. A lifetime, on this account, is measured by its achievements. Time that contributes nothing to the sum of human achievement is time wasted. But the six pieces that measure out Hsieh's life as an artist achieve nothing. At the end of each period of self-imposed privation, all he can say for himself is that he kept going, that he is still alive. There is nothing else to show for his labours. They are, almost by definition, a waste of time. And Hsieh himself would be the first to agree. 'I have been working hard at wasting time,' he declares.

Yet through all this, he has remained alive. Is living, then, a waste of time? Are all the animals that inhabit the earth, with no purpose in life save to keep themselves going, wasting their time? Well, yes, according to Hsieh, because waste for him is a positive thing: it signals not loss and destruction but the promise of freedom, and of growth. Unchained from the tyranny of aims and objectives, from the regimentation of time by the clock and of space by the hard surfacing and walled enclosures of the built environment, the imagination can take flight, escaping through the cracks like air through a ventilator or water through leaky pipes. Hsieh was already onto this when, in an early piece dating from 1973, he began to photograph the streaks and runs of tar spilled on paved ground in the mundane processes of road repair. This was wasted tar – tar that had overflown the rigidity of the hard-surfaced road. But in its liquid streaks and swirls, it had come to life. Substitute time for tar, and you have the essence of Hsieh's later pieces. The time that comes to life, for him, is the time that escapes: time without purpose, without destiny. Hsieh shows us how freedom may be found in the un-destining of time.

But it is not easy. To stay afloat – to evade capture by the physical, societal and institutional structures that threaten both to rein life in and to subject freedom to the discipline of law and reason – requires a huge effort of will. That's what Hsieh means when he says that wasting time, during the execution of his pieces, was hard work. If the willpower is insufficient, or overwhelmed by contrary forces, then the consequences can be catastrophic. Hsieh had already learned this the hard way, from his early 'jump piece', which he freely admits today to have been an act of sheer folly. What was he thinking when he threw himself out of that second-storey window? Did he really believe he could defy the force of gravity? Here, the line of escape was brutally cut short by the hard surface of the urban fabric. Hsieh's brush with the law, while living as a vagrant in New York, briefly threatened an equally brutal interruption, in the form of forcible arrest and detention. Life, as his experience shows us, hangs by a thread. Like those streaks of tar on the pavement, its lines are fragile and delicate. It calls for the utmost care and attention.

There is a fundamental difference, then, between the hard surfaces of the city – upon which its buildings stand, its transport rolls and its walled-in citizens go about, without friction and confident of support – and the surfaces threaded by the lives that wander almost invisibly through the gaps and cracks in the fabric. To inhabit surfaces of the latter kind is to share them with the manifold non-human kinds for which they offer not a solid foundation but an uncertain foothold. To walk them, as Hsieh did in his year of traipsing the ground of New York City, is like balancing on cobwebs; it requires constant vigilance not to lose one's balance and to fall. The balance is between the atmosphere of the city and its earth, even between life and death. Contrary to the indifference of modern metropolitan living, the attention of the wanderer is continually drawn towards the ground as a place to sleep, to rest, to wash, to make a fire. But these are also places of life: where earth and water, bursting through the paving that otherwise seals the city, can meet and mingle with wind, rain and sunshine.

Does this difference in the surfaces of the city have its counterpart in forms of time? Perhaps the title of the exhibition of Hsieh's art at the 2017 Venice Biennale provides a clue. It was called *Doing Time*. This can be read in two senses, and the ambiguity was deliberate. One is the sense of the prisoner, who in 'doing time' is serving a sentence imposed by a court of law. Life itself, Hsieh has declared – in one of his more enigmatic but oft-repeated pronouncements – is a 'life sentence'. But in the other sense, to do time is actively to waste it, to live and to grow, and to find in both a freedom without destiny. While time in the first sense is as hard and immovable as a paved surface, in the second it is fluid and fugitive, affording, like the cracks in the pavement, a line of flight. When Hsieh was about to begin his year of punching the factory time clock, he shaved his head. But as the year dragged on, his hair grew back, longer and longer, until by the end it reached his shoulders. There was clock-time and hair-time. And if the former imposed a sentence, the latter always escaped.

This leads, finally, to the abiding paradox of Hsieh's life and work. It concerns the relation between life and art. Are they separable or inseparable? Can one, or can one not, make a distinction between art-time and life-time? If doing art is wasting time, and if to waste time is to live, then it surely follows that art and life are indeed indistinguishable. In an interview with Adrian Heathfield, Hsieh himself admits that in the piece with the time clock, he 'tried to bring art and life together in time.' Later in the interview, Heathfield suggests that this might be one reason why the art world finds Hsieh's work so difficult to assimilate: 'it is so absolute in its dissolution of art into life.' But to Heathfield's astonishment, Hsieh disagrees. 'I don't really blur art and life,' he responds; 'the pieces themselves are art time, not lived time. . . . my life has to follow art.'[3] That is why the one-year 'rope piece', during which Hsieh was forcibly conjoined to a fellow artist active in the affairs of the art world, turned out to be so unsatisfactory. It blurred the distinction between life and art that he was struggling so hard to sustain, and ultimately propelled him into the paradox of his next piece, founded on the premise that he could only do art, and maintain his integrity as an artist, by refusing to have anything to do either with artists or with the world in which they operated.

But there is life after art. For Hsieh is no saint, and has no pretensions to be one. He has not sacrificed his life to art. Like any prisoner, he has looked forward to release. With the art done, he can get on with life. He is still serving his life sentence, of course, but then so are the rest of us who find ourselves, through no fault of our own, cast upon this earth. The sentences of art are self-imposed, those of life are not. Even the artist, after all, is human.

THE AGES OF THE EARTH

Introduction

Humans have had much to say, over the years, about the formation of the earth in which they find themselves. Latterly, they have even invented a branch of science, namely geology, dedicated to its study. Yet the earth, it seems, has had little to say about humans. Indeed it has been notably quiet on the matter. But if humans can study the earth, why can't the earth study humans? It is not as though study is possible only for creatures gifted, as humans are, with intellectual powers of language and reason. After all, living beings of all sorts attend to each other's ways in the prosecution of their lives. There is sensing, movement and imagination in the cat's study of the mouse, laced with predatory intent, just as much as in the mouse's study of the cat, in crafting its tactics of evasion. Plants, too, are not only deeply attentive to the movements of the sun and winds, and of creatures that come to feed or to pollinate; they also communicate their experience among themselves.

Yet surely, you will object, we should draw the line at animate creatures. Rocks and stones, rivers and glaciers, mountains and seas: these things are utterly insensate. They cannot listen or respond. But many people around the world would disagree, and who's to say that we are right and they are wrong? The Tlingit people, native to a region of the northwest Pacific coast that is home to some of the most active glaciers in the world, insist that glaciers can listen, and can hear what people say of them. It's best to be mindful in their presence, lest they take offence and surge.[1] The Tlingit, be it noted, are no fools. They don't suppose that glaciers have ears. They do acknowledge, however, precisely what the science of geology denies – that the glacier exists for us, first and foremost, thanks to its phenomenal presence, in a world that is ours as well. It is present in its blinding white light, in its cloying, damp chill, and especially in its explosive cracking sound. And it is by way of its presence that it speaks. Its sound is our hearing. And our listening, by the same token, is the glacier's as well.

What goes for the glacier applies equally to other earthly elements. They echo with the blast, quake and grind of their mixture and composition. Nature is not silent. It may have nothing to say, and were our ears open only to facts and propositions *about* the world, as the protocols of science require, then indeed we would hear nothing. We would be deaf to the gale in the trees, the roar of the waterfall and the song of the birds. For these are propositions that stand only for themselves. They are *of* the world, and it behoves us to attend to them. Today, we face the consequences of our inattention, of consigning earthly things to silence, like objects in a museum, distilled into their pure forms and ordered by the categories of reason. We worry about the loss of habitats, of species, even of glaciers as the earth warms up. But let's not forget that in turning nature into fact and knowledge into interpretation – in breaking off from the conversations of life – these things are already lost to us, if not yet to the world.

The elements of fortune

This essay was originally commissioned by the City of Paris Museum of Modern Art in connection with a new exhibition of works by contemporary French and international artists, drawn from the Lafayette Anticipations Collection.[1] Entitled simply YOU, the exhibition was divided into five sections, each going by the name of an element, namely: metals, waters, fires, airs and earths. The idea was that the juxtaposition of these plural elements would generate atmospheres and microclimates that would speak both to the fractures of our present world, and to the promise of creative rebirth. In my essay, I tried to conjure something of the same spirit.

We used to observe a family custom in our house, every New Year's Eve, whereby we would melt miniature horseshoes made of tin, held in a ladle, over the flames of the living room fire. It's a custom we know as coming from Finland, though it may be common to other nations as well. Each of us would take our turn, with our own horseshoe. As soon as the metal had melted, it would be quickly poured from the ladle into a large bucket of cold water. Instantly solidifying, the tin would congeal into weird and wonderful shapes that, once retrieved from the bucket, would be held up against the light so as to cast shadows on the opposite wall. From these shadows we would tell our fortunes for the year to come.

In this little ritual are brought together earth, metal, fire, water and air. For it is from the earth that we draw metals such as tin; it is fire that turns the metal to liquid; it is water that turns the liquid blobs into congealed shapes; and it is in air that the shapes cast their shadows. What might this chain of events tell us about how these elements are related? Does it present, in microcosm, something of what is going on, at a much larger scale, in the formation of our world? And how are human fortunes bound up with these worldly transformations? Here I offer some reflections on these questions, starting from our horse-shoes. I begin, however, with a note about the elements themselves.

We are most familiar with the theory of the elements, as the fundamental constituents of the material world, that has come down to us from Greek Antiquity. It was the Sicilian philosopher Empedocles, around 450 BCE, who proposed the four elements of earth, air, fire and water, to which Aristotle added a fifth, the quintessential aether, changeless and uncorruptible by any of the other four. Classical Chinese philosophy, however, has given us a quite different theory, known as Wu Xing, which developed under the Han dynasty in the second century BCE. In Wu Xing, the five elements are earth, fire, water, wood and metal. Yet the Chinese *xing*, conventionally translated as 'elements', are more like seasons than substances. Their most fundamental property is movement, or, better, the potential to turn. Wood turns to fire, for example, as spring to summer; fire turns to earth as the wood is reduced to ash. Elements, in Chinese philosophy, exist not in themselves but only in what each does to the others, in a world that is never fully formed but continually in formation.

To list the elements as earth, metal, fire, water and air is, admittedly, to play a degree of havoc with both Greek and Chinese systems. Though earth, fire and water are common to both, their meanings in the two systems are entirely different. From the Chinese, we take metal but not wood; from the Greeks, we take air but lose the aether. Our list is somewhat arbitrary, to be sure, and philosophically hybrid. It speaks, however, to the concerns of our own machinic age in which metal has overtaken wood as the armature of industry, and in which aether, drained of spiritual potency, has been reduced to the vacuity of space. Earth, air and water remain as fundamental to life as they ever were: they are the 'elements' we contend with whenever we are out in the weather, on land or at sea, while fire – burning not wood so much as fossil fuels – has contributed decisively to the warming of our planet.

Scientists, of course, tell us that such talk of elements is obsolete. It is, they say, the stuff of myth and folklore, long since overtaken by advances in chemistry. For them, to refer to the elements means reducing matter to its atomic essences – first listed in the periodic table published by the Russian chemist Dmitri Mendeleyev in 1869 – every one of which is ultimately reducible to specific combinations of still more elementary particles, such as protons, neutrons and electrons, from which its properties are derived. Terms like 'earth' and 'air', and even 'metal', have no place in a modern, scientifically informed worldview. They are categories so vague as to defy definition. Why, then, should we continue to speak of them?

We should hold on to them, perhaps, to recover what is lost in the reduction. They are ways of restoring materials to the phenomenal world – to the world of our experience. This is not a world that can be easily classified. It resists division into categories. Indeed, the fact that elements are indefinable may be precisely why we need them. They are like the characters of stories, temperamental and chameleonic, as much affective as substantial, as much existential as essential, as much a part of us as of the world of which we speak. We know them from the inside, intuitively, in their moods and dispositions, by what they do and by what happens when we deal with them. We know them in the way the fish knows the water, the worm the earth, the bird the air, not as matter objectively weighed and measured, but as the weight and measure of our own existence.

Earth, for example, is rock and soil, but it is also the toil of working with it, in the labour of bodies that move and breathe. But if earth is the heaviness of being that keeps us grounded, then air is the lightness in which we dare to dream. We feel the earth by heaving it, the air by breathing it, the water by drinking it or being soaked in it. Fire is the glowing warmth or the searing heat of flames: we feel the heat of the fire in our bellies and in the malleability of molten metal; we feel the sharp edge of cold metal when it is quenched by water. And it is always at the threshold of the elements, where one is about to turn into the other, that significant moments of transformation occur.

With these thoughts in mind, let me return to our little horseshoes. Real horseshoes, of course, are made of iron, and were traditionally cast at the forge by the blacksmith. Fire and metal were his elements, and he had to bring them together to achieve his results. Our fake horseshoes were made of tin – possibly mixed, illicitly, with lead – and we needed nothing more than a fire in the hearth to melt them. With tin as with iron, however, the ore had first to be extracted. Its presence in the earth is the work of geological ages, whether in the gradual deposition of minerals on the sea-floor, as in the formation of iron in sedimentary rock, or through hydrothermal discharge into veins of igneous rock, as with ores of tin. To extract the metal, the ore had to be mined, crushed and smelted. In the crushing, it would meet water, which sorts the metal-bearing particles from the residual gangue; in the smelting it would meet the fire of the furnace. The tin of our little horseshoes, then, born from volcanic eruptions of many millions of years ago, has since seen the lesser explosions of mine-working, the wash of water and the heat of fire, before fetching up in our house one New Year's Eve. And it is about to meet first fire, and then water, all over again.

We're burning coal in the hearth, and this, like the ore of tin, had to be mined from the earth. It, too, bears testimony to the work of ages, born of the fire of the sun, beating down on ancient forests, fuelling their growth. It is this fire that is released when we burn the remnants of these forests, compacted into coal. Fire and earth, fused in the material of wood, are once more split apart as the coal, bursting into flame, is reduced to ash. When, taking my turn, I rest my horseshoe on the ladle and place it before the fire in the hearth, I re-enact, in microcosm, the encounter of the fire of the earth and the fire of the sun, the first heating the magma that hardened into igneous rock in the formation of the earth's crust, the second powering the flourishing of plant life on its surface. And in that moment of encounter, the tin begins to melt.

Fire and metal amount to a devilish combination, unleashing forces that require exceptional strength of those who deal in them. In many societies, the blacksmith was traditionally both feared and respected for playing the devil at his own game and winning, snatching from the fiery jaws of hell the armour and weaponry to protect ordinary folk from evil, the shares to plough the earth, and shoes to protect their most treasured possessions, their horses, from injury. That's why people would hang horseshoes over their doors, to ward off attack from demonic harbingers of misfortune who would recoil at the power invested in them. Our little horseshoes, of course, have no such power. They are fake – not beaten in the forge but shaped in a mould – and here we are, melting them. Why melt a symbol of protection and security? Perhaps it is to break the mould, to put the past behind us, to offer the possibility of a radically new beginning. It's New Year's Eve, after all!

Full of wonder and anticipation, I watch what happens. My horseshoe begins to melt from the inside, and the first indication is that its outer surface begins to behave like a skin, stretching and deforming as it accommodates the liquefying mass beneath. Gradually, before my eyes, the moulded form dissolves into a silvery blob that wobbles uncertainly, jelly-like, while held together by the forces of surface tension. It seems as expectant as I am. With a rapid movement, I withdraw the ladle from the fire, tip it up and empty the contents into the cold water, ready and waiting in the bucket. For a moment, the blob of tin, in free fall, comes to life and breathes the air of liberation. It can be itself, rather than being forced into a mould. Its bid for freedom, however, lasts but a split second. With a hiss and a splash, the falling tin is instantly suffocated, caught in the contortions of its own escape like the victims of a volcanic eruption, overwhelmed by the flow of pyroclastic ash.

It was the wicked alliance of fire and metal, aided and abetted by the legendary King Coal, that drove the industrial revolution. But water, the very element that brings the earth to life, is the kiss of death for metal. It strangles and corrodes. Entire landscapes are strewn with the rusting hulks of giant machines, very slowly dissolving back into the earth. But metal has its revenge. Washed by water in the tailings of mines, or in great mounds of waste piling up in those parts of the world that have become the dumping grounds for affluence, so-called heavy metals are accumulating in such concentrations as to poison the very earth from which they came. Nothing can grow there. Arsenic, cadmium, chromium, copper, lead, mercury, nickel and zinc: all are benign in minute quantities but lethal in concentration. Yet how can the earth be poisoned by stuff that was originally born of it? The very word 'metal' is derived from the Greek *metalleuein*, meaning 'to mine' or 'to quarry'. What has happened to metal, then, that, having once been obtained by mining or quarrying, liberated by fire and washed by water, it returns to earth in such a toxic form?

Perhaps the answer lies precisely in the chemical reduction that has its conceptual counterpart in the reduction of metal, as an elemental constituent of the phenomenal world, into the atomic 'elements' of the periodic table. By crushing and sorting, washing and filtering, 'metals' have been isolated from metal: material that was once infinitely varied and heterogeneous has been separated and distilled into a multitude of pure forms. Anthropologists have long argued that there is danger in pollution, where things that belong to different categories come into contact or when they confound our conceptual distinctions. Acts of purification, then, serve to sustain the conceptual order by eliminating such contamination. But experience in a post-industrial world tells us otherwise. Pollution may be dangerous, but it is the purification of potential pollutants – their initial isolation from the material matrix prior to recombination or re-release – that is most dangerous of all. So long as stuff is all mixed up it is relatively harmless, but to remix or recombine what has once been separated into pure kinds can unleash forces of terrifying magnitude. We have nuclear explosions to prove it.

Now that what remains of my horseshoe has sunk to the bottom of the bucket, I plunge a bare arm into the water to retrieve it. There it is, a splash caught in the very instant of its formation. Where the standard form of the horseshoe had been imposed on the material through a moulding process, the piece I now retrieve is more like a three-dimensional snapshot: it is the arrested form of a fugitive movement. One end is rounded like a blob, the other breaks into wafer-thin shards. In between, the surface of the piece is folded and crumpled in ways so chaotic as to defy description (Figure 17). How

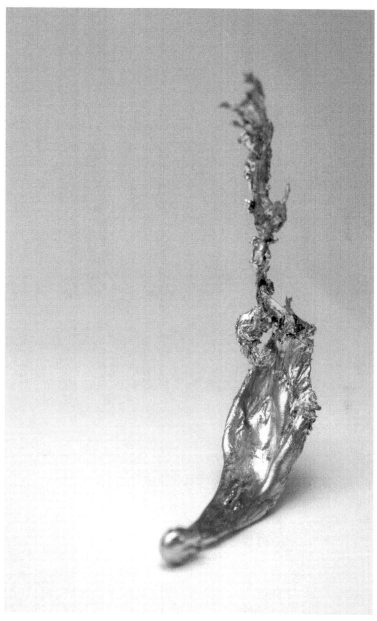

Figure 17 New Year's tin.
(Photo by Tero Sivula, courtesy of Lehtikuva.)

is it possible that, starting with a regular globule of molten metal and a still bucket of water taken from the tap, a singular form of such manifold complexity can emerge? Where does it come from?

For an answer, we might return to the Roman philosopher-poet Titus Lucretius Carus, whose disquisition on 'The Nature of Things' (*De Rerum Natura*) inspired our earlier reflections concerning how, in flight, stillness is held in movement (see pp. 73–4). Every object of perception, Lucretius explains, is precipitated when matter, raining down, deviates slightly from its rectilinear course, setting in train a cascade of collisions.

> . . . when bodies fall through empty space
> Straight down, under their own weight, at a random time and
>   place,
> *They swerve a little.* Just enough of a swerve for you to call
> It a change of course. Unless inclined to swerve, all things would
>   fall
> Right through the deep abyss like drops of rain. There would be
>   no
> Collisions, and no atom would meet atom with a blow,
> And Nature thus could not have fashioned anything, full stop.[2]

But nature fashions many things, among them this strange and singular piece of tin. For I had no hand in shaping it. Its shape emerged as a falling-through-water, in the swerve. It is the form of a cascade. What looks perfectly still to us, as Lucretius surmised, is seething with imperceptible movement. To clinch his point, he asks us to examine the shaft of sunlight pouring through a gap in the shutters. Observe the myriad motes of dust, ever colliding as they dance about, tossed and tumbling this way and that, sometimes clustering, sometimes dispersing. Out of all these motions, he says, normally imperceptible to the naked eye, a world is formed for us to behold. Now's the time, then, to follow Lucretius and to hold our piece of tin to the light.

With this, we finally return to the element of air. Chemically, air may be defined as a mixture of gases, principally oxygen and nitrogen, along with small but increasing quantities of carbon dioxide and methane. It exists for us, however, in our experience, as our capacity to breathe. Likewise, light exists for us not in the form of radiant energy, but in our capacity to see. When we can both breathe and see, there is light and air; when we can do neither, we suffocate in darkness. As walking, breathing beings, we are creatures of both flesh and air, and yet the aerial part of our being – the part that we take into ourselves on the inhalation and give out to our surroundings on the exhalation – is normally invisible. This is because it is transparent. The part we see is the part that blocks the rays of light and casts a shadow.

From the moment when I first placed it on the ladle, I and my piece of tin have become one. Its story is now mine as well. Fishing it from the bucket, I rescued myself from drowning. I held my breath in suspense as the tin sank to the bottom, but now, in the air, I can breathe freely again. And that's my shadow on the wall. I turn the piece this way and that, as if I were examining myself in the mirror. From this angle, how do I look? How about from that one? A story begins to unfold. It's a story that begins as soon as I hold the tin up to the light, but it has no ending. The shadow's changing outlines, blurred by a penumbra, stand for nothing. They are not signs to be decoded. They are uncertain, as I am; their meanings shrouded in the mist. All I can do is to follow the shifting outlines and wonder where they might lead. As I tell my fortune in the shadow-play, the future continually escapes beyond the horizons of my imagination. I cannot pin it down. Telling is finding, not describing what is already found.

Yet even as our fortunes belong to a fugitive future – one of hopes and dreams ever on the point of vanishing into the distance – another kind of future bears down on us, looming closer with every passing year. We measure the speed of life by the distance between this future and our present position: the closer we get to it, the faster we are impelled to act. Like a string that vibrates more rapidly and with a higher pitch the shorter it is, life accelerates, and its sound grows increasingly shrill. We long to slow down. The sense of a future that is coming towards us, rather than speeding away from us, seems to be a peculiar affliction of our present generation. Not only is it the first in human history to experience virtually instant, world-wide communication. It is also witnessing extreme climatic events, coupled with species extinction, on an unprecedented scale. The future, it seems, is already upon us, while our lives are squeezed into the present, bent on immediate gratification.

What would the mighty Empedocles, who gave us the elements of earth, air, fire and water, say were he alive today? Everything in the cosmos, Empedocles had taught, is born of the eternal dialogue of Love and Strife. Within the sphere of Love, all the elements are in accord, but at its outer surface, Strife tears them apart. Looking around, he would indeed observe a world torn by strife: whole mountains ripped open by mining, waters drained to desert, forests aflame, air thick with smog. But he would know, too, that the elements work better together than separated. He might pick up an old, rusting horseshoe and observe that although it is the work of strife, forged of beaten metal in the heat of the fire, its rounded form speaks of love, albeit not yet closed and consummated. He might then throw it, as he is alleged to have thrown himself, into the raging crater of Mount Etna. Legend has it that Etna spat out one of Empedocles' bronze sandals, revealing his claim to immortality to be a hoax. We, too, are mortal, and thanks to being so, we can hope and dream. Immortals, having no future and no past, can do neither. Perhaps, if Etna were to melt the horseshoe and spit it out, recast in the movement of its own ejection, we could read our fortune in it.

We can no longer, however, read our fortunes in tin. In 2018, the European Union banned the manufacture and sale of tin horseshoes, on the grounds that the tin, especially when mixed with lead, is harmful both to the environment and to human health. In the purification of the elements, our hopes have turned to poison. To save ourselves and the earth in which we dwell, must we then forgo the chance to dream? Must we plan, with Empedocles, for immortality?

A stone's life

During a visit to Sicily in October 2016, for an academic conference, I had the opportunity to visit the ruins of Selinunte, on the southwestern coast of the island. I found myself wandering around what had once been a sizeable city, with wide streets, scores of houses and no fewer than five temples. From ancient sources, we know the city was founded in the seventh century BCE by Greek colonists, who mingled with Phoenicians and native Sicilians. But its subsequent history was turbulent, and in 409 BCE it was overrun by a vast army from Carthage. Of its citizens, some 16,000 were slaughtered, 5,000 captured and 2,600 managed to escape. After that, the city passed repeatedly in and out of Carthaginian control. Finally, around 250 BCE, during the Punic wars, and faced with imminent defeat by Rome, the Carthaginians retreated, destroying the city in their wake. Over the following centuries it was largely reduced to rubble, thanks to a series of earthquakes that hit the region. Some of the temple pillars, however, have since been restored. As I looked at them, and put my hand to their rough, eroded surfaces, I imagined not just the rites but the destruction, both human and seismic, they had seen. If stones could speak, I thought, what stories they could tell!

When, subsequently, I was invited to contribute an essay for a publication of the Zadkine Museum in Paris, entitled Being Stone, or Être pierre, *to accompany an eponymous exhibition of stone sculptures,[1] I decided to take up the story of one particular stone from Selinunte. The story is in two parts. In between, I offer some reflections of my own, on the matter of sculpture.*

Figure 18 *Selinunte – Ruins*, a photograph by Giovanni Crupi, dating from the 1880s or 1890s.

I

Long, long ago much of the earth was undersea. In warm and shallow regions, the waters teemed with life. And where there was life, there was also growth, not just of soft, organic tissues but also of the skeletal materials and faecal secretions exuded from them. The detritus of tiny foraminifera, corals, algae and much more continually rained down upon the seabed, forming layer upon layer of calcareous material. As the seas dried, these layers hardened and fused into solid rock. Squeezed by the movement of great continental plates, driven by the tectonic circulations of the earth's crust, the rock was folded into mountains, riddled by waters, gouged by ice. Life reappeared, this time terrestrial rather than marine: plants, animals, finally people. And that's where I come in.

I am the resurrection of life's old bones, born into another time. I am of the flesh of my mother, the gestating earth; and of the seed of my father, the ancient sea. I was delivered in a quarry. It was not an easy birth; they had to hack me out. There were men – many men – who came with metal tools. First they drew a circle, some two metres in diameter. Then they chiselled down along the line to make a groove of equal depth. Undercutting from all around the base of the groove, they finally broke through, brought in levers to haul me up, wrapped me in a great wooden drum and rolled me overland behind a team of oxen to where they were building.

Here I found myself among many of my kind, of similar size and shape. Using hoists, the men were piling them one upon the other to form massive, rounded columns. Eventually my turn came. A huge force kept pulling me down, as if my mother, the earth, would not let me go. With a gaping hole where I had been, her belly emptied, she called after me with a cry so strangled it made no sound. I heard only the bellows of the oxen and the shouts of men, as they struggled and heaved with their machinery to lift me up. At last I found myself laid atop another like myself, high up in the air. The hot rays of the sun, the swirling winds: these were new to me. Was this what it meant to live?

The first thing I had felt, however, was heaviness. I felt it at the very moment I was born, when they cut me free and began to lift. Weight came to me at that turning point, when I realized I could never regress into the matrix whence I had come. For what is weight, if not the pull of the earth for her offspring to return? The more intense the desire for reunion, the harder it is to bear the irrevocability of loss. I had known mass before: it was the sense I already had of being a thing of substance, a composition of materials. I owe my mass to my parents, to the earth and the sea. But weight – that was something altogether different. It was the pain of separation, a pain we suffered together, we orphans of the quarry. We were like acrobats, balanced on each other's shoulders. The stone beneath me carried my burden, augmented by the burden I carried, of all those above.

We bore these burdens without complaint, for hundreds of years, while men worshipped their gods, dreamt of power and immortality, performed their sacrifices and fought their wars. They continued with their quarrying, and raised more columns. And then, in a single day, they disappeared. In terror, they downed tools and fled the quarry, fled their temples, fled their homes. We stood there amidst the clash of arms, amidst the screams. It is said that 16,000 men, women and children were butchered that day by invading Carthaginian troops, while we looked on in silence.

That's not what brought us down, however. It was several centuries later. For down below, the plates were still moving. The earth was creaking under the strain. Something had to give, and finally it did. With one mighty heave, the bedrock snapped along a fault, sending shock waves far and wide. The ground shook violently: for a brief moment I was hurtled from side to side and then I tumbled, landing askew in a great heap, with others beside me, or leaning on me, as I leant on them. We were hung over like drunks after a party, finally released from the eternity of having to stand to attention. I may have looked a bit the worse for wear, but it was a joy to relax in such company, once again to come close to the earth and to feel the warmth of its embrace.

I had all the time in the world to get to know my neighbours: not just the stones that lay beside me but also the weeds and grasses that grew around or even in my crevices, and the little lizards that crawled beneath me for shade or basked in the sun on my skyward-facing surfaces. The people returned as well, albeit not in such numbers. They came not to worship or fight but to draw and paint; they would walk around us as though lost in contemplation, and sometimes would sit on us. They seemed particularly fascinated by the texture of our surfaces, and I was no exception. Many would approach to place their hands upon me, to touch and feel the texture with their fingers and palms.

II

Surfaces? Where do they come from? How are they formed? Surely the stone had no surfaces before it was born, only substance. It's the same with weight and mass. The stone, by its own account, had always known mass but felt weight only in the pain of separation from the earth.[2] It was this separation, likewise, that wrested surfaces from substance. The stone's surfaces were created in violence, by the force of hammer and chisel, in the splitting and rupturing of rock. They had once borne the scars of separation. Yet these wounds are no longer open. In time, the scars have grown over. It is as if the stone were covered by a skin. When people come to touch it, this is what they feel – the skin of the stone. But how can that be? The stone is not like a tree with its bark, nor is it draped in fabric like a human being with clothes. But nor again is it naked, as though its substance was so transparent that human visitors could see right into it, or feel it like dipping their hands into water. So what is this skin, in which our stone is neither wrapped up nor laid bare?

Maybe, taking our cue from John Ruskin (see p. 91), it could be compared to a veil. In the veil, inside and outside are not separated on either side of an impermeable barrier, but are drawn together, where they mix and mingle to form a texture. Inside is mass: a composition of materials drawn from the earth. Outside is atmosphere: the light and heat of the sun; the blast of the wind; occasional but torrential rain. Mass and atmosphere are woven together in weathering. It was in weathering that the stone's surfaces, scarred in the violence of separation, were gradually healed.

We might suppose the weather to be an agent of erosion; that rain, wind and sun only take stuff away. But that's not how it was for the stone. To be sure, the scouring of wind-blown sand, the leaching of rainwater and the illumination of the sun have left it wrinkled and pockmarked, serrated to the touch. But these pockmarks and wrinkles are hardly comparable to the scars of its violent birth. The tools of men tore into its substance and left it broken, but the weather has allowed it to come forth into the fullness of its being. We can read its history and character from the texture of its surfaces, just as, among our own kind, we can read the life-story of a person from the lines and wrinkles of their face and hands. It is surely no accident that speakers of English, at least, and possibly other languages as well, use the same verb, 'to wear', to refer both to the abrasion of weathering and to taking on the veil. Worn hands wear their folds and calluses, the worn face an expression. The stone's texture, worn by the weather, is the veil it wears.

Perhaps this bears on what we mean by sculpture. The artisans who delivered the stone from the quarry, and set it up on a column, were also renowned for their sculpture: their work is still revered today. They carved busts, whole figures and frescoes, with great mastery of technique. Now as a rule, when things are made, materials are added on or joined, one to another. The weaver adds threads, the carpenter joins timbers, the mason piles stone on stone. But sculpture usually works the other way. It is not additive but subtractive. So when the sculptor takes a stone, and carves it, what kind of surface does this create? Is it scarred or veiled?

It is first one and then the other. Attending first to form, the sculptor hews the block. This is to cut transversally, against the grain of nature, as when our stone was initially hewn from the quarry. But then, as more and more material is removed and the form begins to take shape, attention shifts to surface texture. The sculptor's gestures, now less violent, more coaxing, cast a veil on the material, bringing out its sheen. That's when sculpture comes alive. It is as though, in this second stage, the sculptor seeks to imitate the weather. Of course the weather is not the only texture-weaving agent. Think of pebbles on a shingle beach, their rough edges smoothed as they grind each other in the perpetual breaking of the waves, or stones washed up on banks by the river's flood. The sculptor, too, as he grinds and smooths his material, bringing out its texture, goes with the grain of nature, joining in his work with the scouring wind, the roiling sea, the river current, as if to become one with them.

Sometimes, however, people become agents of weathering themselves, without even realizing it. Above all, they weather surfaces with their feet. In temples, in castles and cathedrals, on thresholds, stone staircases and cobbled streets, the passage of countless feet has – over centuries – worn surfaces once rough from the quarry to the smoothness of velvet. The process is so slow that no-one ever notices it. Do you want to know who polished this stone? The answer is that you all did, in the fullness of time.

III

My story did not end with the quake that left me recumbent, lying amidst my stony companions, higgledy-piggledy on the earth. You people who came back to visit us – to draw and to paint – thought us ruined. But you had an oddly two-faced attitude to ruins. You did not know whether to love them or loathe them. For some, of the latter disposition, ruins offended their sense of order. Many of your most eminent philosophers saw a kind of mathematical beauty in the proportions of the ancient temple: a beauty that seemed sacrosanct and timeless, aloof from all the sweat and toil, not to mention the violence, that accompanied its construction, and that I had known so well. They would regard a column and see in it the triumph of reason, not the weight of groaning rock. Their motto was enlightenment. But others professed to a more romantic temperament, seeing in the ruins a kind of beauty they called sublime. In awe of the power of nature to topple the works of men, and revelling in the freedom and exuberance of our manifest disarray, they found in it a source of spiritual solace, a way to restore their being to the world without having to undergo its more material discomforts. For myself, I have no truck with either tendency. When humans reach out to touch me, I do not touch them back. They want to absorb my essence, so they say, but I am indifferent to theirs. Frankly, I couldn't care less. Let humans observe me, touch me and sit on me all they like; none of this will make me any more like them. I am a stone, not an artist or philosopher.

On one fateful day, however, humans of a different stripe arrived on the scene. They were architects and engineers, and came with a word I had not heard before: *anastylosis*. It's Greek for reassembly or rebuilding. They surrounded us, holding up detailed maps and plans, and began to speak in earnest about how we might be restored to our original positions, before the earthquake. 'History can be rewound,' they said. 'We can get the temple back to how it looked before. It will be magnificent!' I and my companions watched in horror as workmen arrived to carry out their instructions. Our thousand-year hangover was about to come to an ignominious end. But we were hardly fit for purpose. All that weathering, not to mention the chips and breakages incurred when we fell, had taken its toll. 'Try putting us one atop the other,' we protested, 'and it will be like balancing a pile of pebbles. The slightest tremor of the earth will bring us down again.' But the men had a solution. '*Concrete*,' they cried. 'We will bond you together with concrete. It is the answer to everything. You will never fall again!'

Why did I have such a strange feeling of affinity when I saw the men opening their big, heavy bags, filled with a mysterious, fine grey powder? And what was this premonition as the powder was poured into great rotating drums, filled with sand and water? Could it have been a twinge of recognition, a vague recollection of how my own life had started underwater, in the mixture of sea sand and powdered bone? Was I coming full circle, back to the future?

Truly, I was peering into the abyss. For what I witnessed, in those bags, was the destruction of the earth and the annihilation of its offspring. The stuff had begun in the same way that I had, as layers of undersea sediment, hardened into rock. Like me, it had been forcibly extracted at the quarry. But thenceforth its fate had been entirely different from mine. For no sooner had it left the quarry than it was smashed to pieces, crushed and pulverized. It could never feel its weight or present its surfaces. It never had a chance to live. Its fate was rather to be cremated, cast into the fires of a furnace, only to emerge red-hot, as balls of clinker fused by the intense heat. Once more crushed and ground into the finest dust, it filled the bags the men were now emptying into their mixing machine, from which emerged a semi-liquid slurry. This was the magic ingredient that would fill the gaps where the pieces of the three-dimensional stone jigsaw were missing or didn't quite fit.

Many people complained. It is an anachronism, they said, to mix this modern material with ancient stones. The stones have texture, they bespeak the past. But concrete is bland, homogeneous and devoid of history. It doesn't belong. Well, I wouldn't disagree with that; it's what I've always said myself. But things are not so bad, after all. We're back up now, in our columns, once more standing to attention. I'm so high up that no humans can touch me, but the birds and insects fly by, and I can feel the wind and the sun. Moreover, I don't much mind the concrete that fills my cracks and joints. After all, it is cousin to me, and no more chose its fate than I did. We have fun arguing about which of us will last the longest. Concrete is full of itself: it has been wholly taken in by the propaganda of its manufacturers. 'I am the new magic stone,' it says. 'I am harder, stronger, more powerful. For every modern temple-builder, I'm the material of choice. For I can take on any form you like, and it will last forever.'

Yet I know these are empty boasts. You cannot speed up time, I say. It is true that I share concrete's watery origins. But think how many millennia it took for my layers to form and solidify, and think, too, how slowly my surfaces are worn – at a rate almost imperceptible on the human scale of time. So what does concrete say? That it takes not millennia but just a few days to harden into a rock so solid it will never wear!

It's a myth to think that stone can be created in an instant. The fact is that concrete never really dries. The water stays inside, binding with sand and cement. That's why all concrete is bound to crumble, sooner or later. When it does, we stones will fall again. People will come and observe the ruins. The lizard will sit in the sun, the grass will grow between the cracks, and I will ever pine for the earth from which I came. Perhaps one day, the warming created by all those cement furnaces, and the fossil fuels they burn, will cause the ocean levels to rise, and I'll find myself back where I started, beneath the waves. Gradually, I will be covered by the detritus of the sea and will end my days as a fossil, not raised in the air but buried deep in the earth, stone within stone. Finally, I will have found my way home.

The jetty

Catalyst *is the title of a volume featuring the work of the sculptor Wolfgang Weileder.*[1] *The volume grew from a project focusing on the jetty of Dunston Staiths, one of a number of derelict structures originally built along the banks of the River Tyne, near Newcastle, to facilitate the transfer of coal from rail to ship. The Jetty Project combined Weileder's experimental approach to using recycled materials in performances of building and dismantling with the work of his principal collaborator, sociologist Simon Guy, in urban planning and sustainable architecture. I was invited to write a foreword to the volume, and chose to focus on the work entitled* Cone, *a round, turret-shaped construction made from blocks of the material Aquadyne, manufactured from recycled waterborne plastic. Aquadyne harvests the marine deposit of human manufactures for use on land, in a precise reversal of the extraction of naturally formed and landlocked deposits of coal for maritime use as fuel for steamships. Weileder's* Cone *brings together the stories of coal – of its geological formation and of the men who went on to mine it – with the stories of their descendants, surrounded by industrial decline, ruination and waste. In this work, the respective weights of coal and plastic, and of a past of extraction and a future of recycling, are folded into one another in a powerful assertion of a mode of sustainability that lies not in the final achievement of a steady state but in always building, unbuilding and rebuilding.*

How heavy is the past? You might suppose that it doesn't make much sense to weigh history in tons, as you might weigh sacks of coal. Though we may say of the past that it weighs heavily on the mind, or that it places its own burdens on the present, these are surely figures of speech whose expressive force lies in the way they lead us to draw parallels across what, from the start, are distinct domains of reality. Is coal not literally weighty? Rock solid, it has been hacked from the earth and raised against the force of the earth's gravity. By comparison, the weightiness of the human past strikes a metaphorical chord. Its accumulation is insubstantial; its pull affective rather than gravitational. One, it seems, belongs fair and square to the material domain; the other depends on sedimentations of memory that can only be attributed to a mind. Far from dissolving the division between mind and matter, the metaphor appears to reinforce it. It is a division that has plagued philosophy for centuries.

Arguably, it is the same with sustainability. This is a matter to which the engineers and construction workers who built the massive wooden jetty of Dunston Staiths, in Gateshead, must have given much thought. Built to despatch mined coal into ships for onward transport by sea, the jetty had to be strong enough to bear the weight of a locomotive and a train of loaded wagons. Today, more than three decades since the last ship sailed from the Staiths, the jetty has once again become a focus for thinking about sustainability. The argument, however, is no longer about the physical load it will carry, but about its capacity to bear the weight of the past. For only a present that can sustain the past from which it was forged, and the responsibilities that go with it, can offer a foundation for the future. Can the jetty bear this weight? Will it continue as a living presence in the minds of the people, or will it survive only as a relic, as the memories of its heyday pass?

What has brought these questions to a head is not the efficient discharge of coal but the presence of a work of art. Now, you might think that a million miles separates the weight of coal from the weight of the past, and a railway wagon from an artwork. The coal-filled wagon puts the jetty's sustainability to test in a manner that could hardly be more concrete. The cost of failure would be immediate, physical collapse. The artwork, by contrast, appears to present a more abstract and conceptual challenge to its sustainability. No dire material consequences would attend its failure, no destruction of livelihood, no threat to life and limb. But I do wonder whether the distance between the wagon and the artwork, in the ways they question the capacity of the jetty to sustain the weight of coal in the one case and the weight of the past in the other, is as great as we imagine. Is it really as unbridgeable as that between literality and metaphor, or between matter and mind?

The heaviness of coal, after all, is not simply given, as an objective property of the stuff itself. With coal as with any other material, heaviness – the heft of things – is not so much measured as *felt*. It is felt in the force of compression that one mass, cut from its earthly matrix, exerts upon another. Coal does not weigh so long as it is left in the ground. But its weight was undoubtedly felt by the bodies of miners, as they hacked and shovelled, and by the timbers of the jetty, groaning under the load. Yet if weight is felt, so too is thought as it wells up in the imaginative consciousness of being. Intention and 'in tension': are they not one and the same? Do weight and thought, then, really lie on opposite sides of the divide between matter and mind, or are they rather unified, at a more fundamental level, in the movement of things' feeling-for-one-another? For when all is said and done, matter is the mother of us all: life is forged, as are ideas conceived, in the turbulence of materials.

If the heaviness of thought lies in the histories that have shaped our lives, so, likewise, the heaviness of coal is the product of its geological past. Formed from ancient forests, coal stores up all the energy of the summer sun that once bore down on trees in leaf, year in year out, fuelling their woody growth. For almost a century, that coal held the potential to produce the future: a future which, compared with what had gone before, carried the promise of material prosperity. That future is now past. It was unsustainable. The artwork, Wolfgang Weileder's *Cone*, promises an alternative (Figure 19). The work is built up from slabs of a material as black as coal, as heavy as coal, and extruded – as coal is – from the sediment of the past. But this past is recent, for the material, known as Aquadyne, is made from the kind of plastic waste currently choking our oceans and filling our lands. Might these deposits, at some time in the future, serve as standing reserves of raw material for the manufacture of Aquadyne, which, by then, could be as ubiquitous as concrete is for us now?

Figure 19 *Cone*, by Wolfgang Weileder, 2014.
(Photo by Colin Davidson.)

It is above all in the making of the work, in its performance, that the past and materials weigh together. The forefathers of those very apprentices who found employment in building *Cone* would, in their prime, have been mining coal, or shovelling it, or discharging it into the chutes that released it to the waiting ships. And as their present-day descendants stacked up the slabs of Aquadyne, this long-overlooked past would once again have bubbled up in stories which told of bygone times even as they imagined times to come. It is not, then, that slabs weigh literally – a total of 11 tons, to be exact – while the past weighs metaphorically. In performance, the respective weights of the past and of the slabs are felt equally, at the same time. And here's another thing about performance: you could just as well be unmaking as making, putting things together as taking them apart. Coal is hacked from the rock-face only to fill the wagon, and the wagon is filled only for it to be emptied. And true to form, *Cone* was erected only to be taken down, following which its slabs are to be reused elsewhere.

Finally, consider the structure. Thrust out into the tidal waters of the River Tyne, the jetty is a one-way thing (Figure 20). It is not like

Figure 20 The jetty at Dunston Staiths, Gateshead.
(Photo by Colin Davidson.)

a bridge, which allows passengers safe crossing to another shore from which they may just as safely return. For the coal that was rolled out onto its platform, there was no way back. Shipped to an unknown future, it had no recourse to the past. The wagons, however, came and went, as indeed artworks can if they are built first here, then there. It is the same with scaffolding: it goes up and comes down. I sometimes wonder, of buildings, whether we should think of them at all as finished structures. Perhaps they, too, are really scaffolds for the life process that unfolds in them. And this, surely, is what Weileder wants us to see with *Cone*. In art as in architecture, sustainability is about keeping life going, not about hovering around an interminable equilibrium. And as long as the tides wash in and out, as birds nest in the nooks and crannies of the Staiths, and as people come to tick them off in their books, time will keep passing, ever so slowly, on its course.

On extinction

Responding to an invitation from the editors of the journal The Clearing, *to contribute to a collection of essays on the theme of extinction, it had never been my intention to write a poem. However, as I was thinking about it on the short walk I take daily before breakfast, words began to come into my mind and arrange themselves with a rhythm and cadence that must have corresponded with the lilt of my steps. Back at the breakfast table, I quickly wrote down the lines I already had. It seemed only natural, once under way, to continue in the same vein. The result was this poem, which I have revised slightly since its original publication.*[1]

Extinction is for others, not for us. We'll never know
What words turned out to be our last, what steps we took
Into the abyss. For who will say of humans:
'Remember them? They went extinct,'
As now we say of woolly mammoths or Neanderthals?

Will historians among the animals
Write letters on the shifting sands, or in the roots of trees,
To say that there were people once, before they disappeared?
Will canine fossil-hunters, rooting in the undergrowth,
Scenting a tooth, or the fragment of a skull,
Bark the finding of another hominin?
Or will the mole turn silent archaeologist
To dig up its remains?

Will raucous gulls, preferring cities to the sea,
Cry over the loss of their inhabitants,
Or just take up inside the ruins?
Will the worm regret the passing of the farmer,
Or fish the angler's hook and line?
No doubt they'll carry on without us
As once they did before we came.
They're really quite indifferent.

But in a world that still has elephants,
Why should mammoths be extinct?
Or Neanderthals, in a world that still has humans?
Could not elephants be the mammoths of today, and humans the
    Neanderthals?
'No no,' we say, 'mammoths are not elephants,
And Neanderthals are not the same as us.
They were another race of humankind,
Wiped out by our superior ancestors!'

That's also what the white men said,
On wiping out the people of Tasmania.
'They're just another race,' they said, 'and we're superior!'
But they came back, the people:
'You are us,' they said, 'and we're still here.
We're all mixed up, you see, there are no races.'
Was it any different in the Palaeolithic?

For here's the question: if mixed-up-ness is the way we are,
If life itself runs in and out of things just like the air we breathe,
And will not be contained,
Then nothing goes extinct, lest all does.
So how can we remain, while others go extinct?

Yet that's not how we tend to think of it.
The story of extinction is one that we alone are wont to tell.

A story of a world divided, each species for itself,
Competing with the rest for limited resources.
For one to go, and another to survive,
They must be set apart.
There's no extinction, then, without distinction.

Yet we who tell this tale have turned our backs upon the world
And classified its contents as if they were for us alone,
Not we for them. We've made of nature a museum,
A cabinet of curiosities, its contents ordered, sorted, classified,
And made ourselves the keepers of it.
Far from caring for it, though, as good curators would,
We've rampaged through the drawers, spreading mayhem,
And squandered most of our collection.

These kinds, however, that we're about to lose . . .
Has not the life departed from them first?
Are they not already, in a sense, extinguished?
It seems we've dealt a double death, first by locking every beating
      heart,
Each flying, walking, swimming, growing thing,
Into the prison of a drawer; second, then,
By terminating its line. That line is not of life but of descent,
Along which nothing grows. It's not a movement but a chain,
Each link the devolution of a form, as if it could be parted from its
      growth.
Yet form apart from growth is death; in life there's but a process of
      formation.

How can you extinguish what's been put to death?
There must be something to put out,
Light, life, love, hope, a flame, a fire.
It has to burn, to have a movement to it,
A swelling or concrescence.
But species, heading for extinction, no longer have their lives to live.

They're nothing but their genes, a treasure trove of heritable
   information,
Biodiversity. We're losing it, we say. But the life's already lost.
It went with the partition of the world.

Three short fables of self-reinforcement

The anthropologist Bronislaw Malinowski famously described social life as a long conversation, a toing and froing that carries on indefinitely. But there is no reason why the conversation should be limited to human beings, or even to living things. Nor need humans be at the centre of it. In the long-term scheme of things, they might have no more than a walk-on part, making a brief appearance and then disappearing again, while the sun and the moon, the wind and the tides, earth and sea, trees and rivers, carry on regardless. At a time when scientists have declared the advent of a new geological era, the Anthropocene, in which human activity is judged to be the dominant force in shaping the earth, we are also more than ever troubled by the thought that human life may soon have run its course on the planet, and that little can be done to prolong our stay. Whatever comes after the Anthropocene is unlikely to include a significant human presence. We are caught, it seems, in a spiral of what the physicist Walter Behrmann, writing a century ago, called 'self-reinforcement'.[1]

In what follows, I have responded to Behrmann's text, on the invitation of the editors of the four-volume compendium Grain, Vapor, Ray: Textures of the Anthropocene.[2] *Each allegorical tale recounts a conversation: of sea-sand with wind, of river with tree, of humans with their built environment. The first two conversations end up in a kind of settlement, or at least a perpetual stalemate; the third, however, leads to oblivion. It is the fate that inevitably awaits us if, instead of joining with* the world, we strive – by ever more massive feats of engineering – to defend ourselves *against* it. Self-defence is ultimately self-destruction.

I

A shell lies on the beach. Once it had housed a living mollusc that had found a place upon the rocks, and had fed itself by filtering particles of nutriment washed over in the ebb and flow of the tides. For this it had the moon to thank. But now, stranded under the relentless glare of the sun, empty and lifeless, holed and fractured by collisions with the shingle, it awaits its end. Eventually, it knows, it will be ground into the self-same sand upon which it now rests: the ever-accumulating deposit of countless others who have met the same fate. Yet up above, the air is growing restless. Moist vapour, warmed by the ground, is rising and – meeting with little pressure from higher layers – is cooling as it goes, condensing into clouds which blot the sun and diffuse its rays. The little shadow that the shell had cast upon the sand disappears. A sudden coolness causes a party of human beachcombers, who had been wandering along the shore, to huddle up. One of them, who had been on the point of retrieving the shell and pocketing it as a memento, thought better of it and left it untouched. How differently things would have turned out had he picked it up!

The clouds, dense with moisture, turn grey and threatening. Along comes the wind – just a gentle breath at first, enough to scuttle a few grains here and there. A stronger puff follows, then stronger still. Soon the puffs become a howl. Our humans run for shelter. Save for the shell, the beach is deserted. The wind, it seems, has taken command of an almost empty kingdom.

'I blow, therefore I am,' proclaims the wind, haughtily, as it sweeps over the shell, scarcely pausing in its passage. 'You, little shell, are nothing to me!' it bellows. 'I can tear down trees and whip the sea into giant waves. I can demolish houses and sink ships. Why, those very waves that cast you up upon the shore: I caused them.' The shell cowers: it has not encountered this mighty force before. Tossed in the waves, it had known the turbulence of the sea, but not the reason for it.

But when the gust has passed, the shell feels an irresistible urge to scratch. Something is tickling it. Though beaten in the face by the heavier of the grains of sand the wind had hurled against it, some finer grains seem to have landed on its back. Some, whipped up by the wind in its passage, have been casually discarded on the lee side. But others have been pulled in from behind. For in sweeping over the summit of the shell, the wind had left a void, and the undertow of air that rushed to fill it had deposited grains in its wake. Along comes the wind again, and where the initial irritation had been, something begins to swell. The swelling grows and grows. Before long, a little mound is formed.

'I blow, therefore I am,' proclaims the wind, condescendingly, as it sweeps over the mound, briefly pausing in its passage. 'You, little mound, are almost nothing to me,' it adds. But nevertheless, it feels some momentary hindrance as though, forced upwards, it has to slow its pace a little. And as it slows, its grip slackens – ever so slightly – letting slip a few more grains. And with every grain, the mound rises. Soon it shows up as a conspicuous bump on the beach.

'I blow, therefore I am,' proclaims the wind again, more in hope than in glory, as it thrusts into the upward slope of the mound. But it needs a big push to overtop the summit, and having done so, with one big sigh, it releases its entire load of windborne sand, which goes sliding and tumbling down on the other side. Then the mound addresses the wind:

'You wind – you who created me – are indeed your blowing. When you do not blow you are nothing. I cannot catch you, or put you in a bottle and say, "There, inside that bottle, lies the wind." You cannot, like the shell, become a collector's item. I lay a trap for you, and you vanish. But I stand my ground. When you cease your blowing, I am still here, until perhaps the rain or the spring tide washes me away. For whilst you are all movement, I am all settlement. You shriek; I slumber. Your shapes are eddies in the swirl of time; mine are heaps that have fallen out of it. You are history; I am archaeology. Your cessation is my formation. I last and am lasting; you are ephemeral. You boast of how you can uproot trees, sink ships and destroy buildings. But with me it is the other way around: the harder and longer you blow, the higher I rise. You try to blow me down and my strength only increases. Indeed, I am invincible!'

At this, the wind is mightily provoked. 'I suppose you think,' it says to the mound, 'that you can just go on rising, up and up, until you reach the sky. The truth is that you rise up only because the grains which make you are continually falling down. Your form is nothing but a perpetual state of collapse. My strength is your inertia.' And with that, the wind again begins to blow, stronger and stronger. As it does so, it whips off the sand from the summit of the mound, scattering it far afield. Soon, the mound begins to flatten out until, once again, more sand is deposited by the wind as it ascends than is blown off from the top.

For ever after, the wind and the mound have carried on their argument, fought with vapour and with grains. They know now that neither side will win, and have called an uneasy truce. And that's how our party of humans find them now, as they reappear on the beach. Human beings – especially the children among them – love to dig, and one of them begins to excavate the mound. As she delves deeper and deeper with her spade, as though searching for buried treasure, another mound is formed. As in all human endeavours, digging down means building up, and building up means digging down. Only if we dig, only then can we build. And the ground? It is simply the difference between the two, where rising and falling cancel each other out.

As for the shell that started it all: if you dig down far enough, you might just find it. But most likely it will already have broken into smithereens, no longer distinguishable from the sand with which it was once surrounded.

II

Once there lived a tree. It had grown close to a riverbank, and the current of the river, as it dragged the bank, had exposed many of its roots. Sometimes, in times of flood, these roots would be submerged, and the trunk surrounded by water. But it was the wind that eventually brought the tree down, during a great storm that devastated the woods. Having toppled towards the stream, the roots were left high and dry while the trunk and branches were now submerged, bent and beaten by currents of water rather than wind. Not that the river's flow was completely blocked, since the fallen tree extended only halfway across to the opposite bank, and there was room for the water to find its way around the new obstruction. Moreover, even where they lay, the trunk and branches formed only a partial barrier. They slowed the flow but did not stop it altogether.

As it lay there, the tree wistfully recalled bygone days. It remembered how, as a little sapling sporting its very first leaves, it had taunted its elders and betters. 'Look at me,' it had said, 'I can catch the light. You can't put me in your shade.' And kindly waving their leaf-heavy boughs, the big trees had replied: 'You will one day grow great and strong like us, but you will eventually fall and rot. No tree stands forever. If the wind doesn't knock you down, then fungi will eat you from the inside, and the woodpeckers will pick at your rotting flesh to feed on the bugs that will inhabit it.'

Every year, without fail, the big trees cast their leaves, rain fell and fungi got to work on the sodden litter, turning it into a rich, nourishing humus. The sapling grew and grew: not by a laborious process of heaping stuff up, as the forest ants were doing in building their nest nearby, but by the extrusion of materials along its grain. For the grain of the tree consists of lines of growth rather than particles of matter, and it is held together by knots rather than by the equilibrating force of gravity. The more it rose in height and expanded in girth, the further its roots extended underground. And the greater was its thirst for light. Wherever a ray of light penetrated the canopy, the tree would set out a leaf to catch it. More leaves meant more humus, more humus meant more root growth, more root growth meant more new shoots and leaf-buds, more leaves meant more energy for growth and more litter to decompose, and so on and on. When would the cycle ever cease?

Well, the gale put an end to that. And here it lay, that once proud tree, humiliated, no longer erect but prostrate, and drenched in an element that it had never known except as rainfall from the sky. The river waters gurgled and chortled all around it, laughing at the tree's ignominy. 'You grow old and die,' they tittered, 'but we are forever young. We never stop running.' The tree was not amused, and as the taunts of the waters surged to a chorus, its humiliation turned to resentment, and its resentment to obduracy. 'You wait,' it said to itself. 'I will teach these waters a lesson they won't forget.' And that is exactly what it did.

As the waters approached, the tree would impede their progress. Slowed down, the waters would inadvertently let loose the dirt they were carrying, washed from the banks and beds of upper reaches. Gradually, a bank of sediment began to build, filling in the gaps between the boughs that had previously allowed the waters through. And as the sediment rose, the waters shallowed, slowing their movement even further due to friction with the bed. The waters following behind were growing increasingly impatient. 'Get moving,' they cried; 'we cannot wait – there's more behind us. Swing out around that tree!' So the waters swung out, only to collide at full force with the bank on the opposite side of the river from where the tree had fallen.

The impact on the bank, however, was enough to send the waters careering back towards the other side. And at the turning point, where the waters were swung around, the bank began to crumble. The constant collision with the waters was wearing it away. The rising sandbank on one side was causing the waters to cut a curve on the other. And further downstream, another curve was being cut on the first side by the waters that were striking it on the rebound. And so on. The waters' once straight descent had become a slalom run. 'Watch me!', cried the waters to the embanked tree as they swooshed by; 'this is cool.' But with each swoosh, their speed slowed. Soon it was reduced to a slack meandering.

The old tree, now high and dry on the sandbank in which it was almost completely embedded, sighed in satisfaction. It had, at length, secured its retribution: not perhaps a resounding victory, but a settling of scores. For the river that had once taunted it with claims of everlasting youth was now condemned forever to wander impotently, this way and that. No longer did it laugh and chuckle. It rather crawled along, sulky and brooding.

That is, until another terrific storm, and the ensuing flood, washed away the sandbank and took the whole tree with it, breaking through the meanders and leaving them as bow-shaped ponds. And the tree? It finally found its way to the sea, where it is floating still, lost among the countless other trunks and boughs cast as driftwood on the oceans. Some wash up on land, and are used by people for fuel or as building material. But others sail the seas forever, or join the wooden ship-wrecks down below. Maybe that is what will happen to our tree, or maybe – washed up on a sandy beach – it will kick-start the formation of another mound.

III

The townspeople were complaining. 'Our streets are clogged with traffic,' they grumbled. 'They were meant for donkeys, not for cars. They are too narrow, they twist and turn, and there's no space for anyone to park. Local businesses are suffering. We need a town plan that is fit for tomorrow's world, not for the world of yesteryear.' After a long campaign, the town's council agreed to do something about it. 'We will widen and straighten the streets,' they said, 'even if it means knocking down a few old buildings. And we will build a bypass for all the traffic that does not want to stop here.'

The people were happy. Big machines arrived: bulldozers, excavators, steamrollers. Men with hard hats appeared. So did the Prime Minister, who put on a hard hat to have his photograph taken for the press. There he was, standing shoulder to shoulder with the construction workers, dressed for the job. 'Our government means business,' people thought. 'We should vote for them!'

After many months, the work was done. The noise subsided; the men and their machines left. The Prime Minister reappeared, no longer in a hard hat but with scissors and red tape. First they closed the road with the tape, after which the PM cut the tape to declare the road open. Everybody cheered, and life carried on.

At first, all went well. Local trade was brisk, and many businesses decided to expand. With limited room in the town centre, they resolved to take advantage of the new bypass to build spacious complexes on the outskirts. The expansion drew in new residents who needed houses. Hastily built estates popped up on low-lying land around the edge of town. The people who came to live there also needed cars to travel to work and to the new shopping centres. The showrooms were busy.

More people, more cars. After a while, the people began to complain again. Instead of racing down the bypass, they found themselves stuck in traffic jams. Rising tempers and fumes from exhaust pipes filled the air. Asthmatic and stress-related conditions were on the rise. 'We need a new bypass,' the people said, 'that will take the through traffic out of our town, as the old one is already clogged. And we need an underground car park in the town centre.' Back came the machines, the construction workers, and the Prime Minister – a different one now – in his hard hat. But this time, the people had something else to complain about.

'We need petrol to drive our cars,' they said. 'But oil supplies are running out, and the price goes up and up. We cannot afford it.' The PM told them not to worry. 'My government,' he said, 'is committed to investment in new technology that will enable us to access unlimited supplies of oil. We will drill holes up and down the land, deeper than have ever been drilled before. And oil will come pouring out of them.'

So they built the new bypass, drilled the holes, brought up the oil. People drove around and life went on. Then the rain came.

First there was just a spot of heavy rain, leading to warnings of difficult driving conditions. But then came more rain, and still more. The Prime Minister returned yet again, to have his photograph taken not with a hard hat, but wearing freshly acquired wellington boots. He waded through the town's streets and sympathized with the residents. He promised that no expense would be spared in cleaning up the mess, once the rain stopped. But money cannot stop the rain. And the rain did not stop.

Some blamed the politicians. Some blamed farmers for putting profit before sense, with agricultural methods that caused increased run-off from the land. Some glanced heavenwards and rolled their eyes. But others argued that exhaust fumes from traffic, having polluted the atmosphere, had turned the weather upside down. Scientists lined up to say that it was all due to anthropogenic climate change, caused by the accumulation of greenhouse gases. And they warned that a tipping point had already been passed. Every increment of warming would only have the effect of releasing gases into the atmosphere or redirecting ocean currents in such a way as to cause further destabilization. The spiral of climate change, they said, was self-reinforcing and irreversible.

The rain kept falling, and the town – now completely underwater – was no longer habitable. The few who had stayed on packed their bags and left. Life went on, but it was always somewhere else.

Many centuries have passed, and you are wandering through a desert landscape, under the hot glare of the sun. For the most part it has been taken over by wind-blown sand, but a few shrubs, adapted to the arid conditions, poke out here and there. And in places, too, the sand has formed small mounds. Digging into them, you sometimes come across a fragment of concrete, a broken brick, a lump of asphalt, rusty metal. 'There were people here once,' you say, 'but we do not know who they were.' And the sand and the wind, absorbed in their everlasting argument, are too busy to notice.

LINE, CREASE, THREAD

Introduction

We began our correspondences deep in the woods. Then, heading for the coast, we embarked on an ascent from the shoreline through hills and mountains to the sky, only to fall back eventually to land. Having alighted there, we turned with the ground, lay low and ventured undercover. We have mingled with the elements in recounting the stories of the earth, throughout the ages, in voices of its own. Our next adventure will take us from these conversations with earthly things to correspondences in words: from ground to page; from walking and flying to writing; from the gathering of leaves in the woods to their binding in the book.

The transition, we discover, is a smooth one. We proceed, without interruption, from the furrows of the ploughed field to the wire of the fence; from the shadow of the wire on the ground to the negative image cast on the blueprint or photographic plate; from the image to its positive, the material thread; and from the looping and twisting of the thread to the oscillations of the letter-line as it weaves its erratic course across the page. No ontological frontier is crossed in the passage from world to words. Yet as we go on our way, we find that the ambience of the outdoors gradually fades. In place of the woods and fields in which we were used to roam we find ourselves indoors, in the familiar surroundings of the study, seated at a desk and writing our lines. From where we sit, the outdoors can only be imagined, or seen through a window. Try as we might to reach out for it, all we can do is leave a scratch-mark on the pane.

Before embarking on the next few essays, however, I advise you to try a simple experiment, which you can very easily do at home. Take a sheet of paper, and rule a straight line across it, in any direction you please. Then screw the paper tightly in your fist. What was once a

Figure 21(a)–(c) Paper sheet with ruled line (a), screwed into a ball (b), and a part of the sheet flattened out (c). (Photos by the author.)

plain, two-sided surface has now become something like a ball, with an irregular, convoluted skin. Your ruled line has been largely swallowed into its innards, though you may see glimpses of it here and there. Next, smooth the paper out again on a flat table-top (Figure 21(a)–(c)). You will find that it has taken on the appearance of a furrowed landscape, with a complex pattern of ridges and valleys. Illuminated from the side, as by a sun low in the sky, light-facing ridges put their leeward faces in the shade, lending a subtly variegated texture to the entire surface. It is a surprise to find how, starting from the simplest of beginnings, a surface of such complexity can emerge. But perhaps most surprising is the fate of the ruled line. For it seems to ride the ups and downs as if it were untouched by them. Has it become its own shadow? Bear this question in mind as you read on.

Lines in the landscape

Much of the land of East Anglia is very flat. Once it was fresh- and saltwater marsh, perilous to those who did not know its ways, and navigable only by watercraft. Over the last several centuries, however, the fens have been drained. The reclaimed land has been turned over to agriculture; rich in minerals, it yields abundant crops. In a stunning series of images, photographer Nisha Keshav has sought to capture the essence of this agricultural landscape, with its great expanses of earth, huge skies and wide horizons. When she asked me to write an introduction to an exhibition of her work, which she had decided to call Lines in the Landscape, *I was intrigued. 'Why lines?' I wondered. One of her photos featured a large, recently ploughed field under a spring sky (Figure 22). The image could be divided roughly into four horizontal strips: in the foreground a yellow-green bed of tall grass, then the rust brown of ploughed earth receding into the distance to give way to a thin dark green band of leafy trees, and – above the horizon marked by the canopy – the blue-giving-way-to-white of a cloud-flecked sky. If you were to copy the picture using only pencil and paper, you might draw the grasses as lots of short upright lines, the furrows of the plough as lines converging towards a vanishing point, and the field boundary and the canopy-horizon as rough horizontals stretching across the sheet. The question is: are any of these lines really there, or do they exist only in the mind's eye? In drawing them, are you merely following a graphic convention that anyone accustomed to perspectival depiction can understand and 'read', or are you participating – in the roaming of your eyes and corresponding gestures of the hand – in the formative processes of the landscape itself?*

Figure 22 Lines in the landscape. (Photo by Nisha Keshav.)

Are there lines in the landscape? Many would say there are not. '*Lines?*
I see no lines,' the great artist Francisco Goya is reputed to have
declared.[1] Observe the furrows of a ploughed field: the surface of
the ground is corrugated, and the angling sunlight illuminates the
ridges on one side while leaving troughs on the other in their shade.
No lines, however, are apparent in the ground itself. Observe the
seedlings growing on the ridges: perhaps we remark that they are
planted along lines, yet it is we who line them up, in our imagination.
The plants themselves, each rooted to a particular spot, have no such
connection. Now observe the trunks of trees: to our sight they might
present limits of occlusion, obscuring from a particular vantage point
what lies immediately behind. We might draw these limits as parallel
lines, yet we know that the actual forms of tree-trunks are variations
on the cylindrical. Even the rungs of a field-gate or electrical cables
appear lineless when you look at them close-up.

So it seems, too, with the fern, the thistle and the reed. In growth,
they reveal a dendritic pattern, but a stem is a stem, a stalk a stalk and

a leaf a leaf – these are not lines. Nor are the ditches that have been cut in the land to drain the fens: straight they may be, but where water meets earth, and mingles with the stems of plants, there are no lines. The edge of a field, where brown earth gives way to green grass, presents a colour contrast, but no line is inscribed there. Cast your eyes towards the sky on a fine, breezy day: the cirrus clouds look feathery, you say, but they are no more composed of lines than are the wings of a bird; the reeds, blown by the wind, all sway in one direction, but directions are abstractions of our own – they are not present in the world. As for the line of the horizon, however far you seek, no more will you find it than the legendary end of the rainbow.

But if there really were no lines in the landscape, then how is it that, equipped with pencil and paper, we can so readily delineate the furrows or boundaries of a ploughed field; the trunks and branches of trees; marching pylons and suspended cables; the stems and leaves of plants; the edges of a ditch or the billowing of a cloud; even the very horizon where, in our perception, the earth appears to meet the sky? And how is it that these features are so instantly recognizable when we show our sketch to a friend who has never before visited the scene? Where do the drawn lines of the sketch come from if there are none to be observed in the world of phenomena? Are they merely in our heads? Can we interpret the sketch only because we share a common set of more or less arbitrary representational conventions that enable us to 'read' straight lines converging upon a vanishing point as furrows, scribble of varying density as foliage, short upright lines as reeds and longer parallels as trunks, and a single straight line dividing top from bottom as the horizon?

Generations of writers and theorists have argued precisely thus. Lines, they say, are a visible expression of the way the human mind cuts up the continuum of nature into regions, objects or entities that can be identified and named. They set things apart: here the land, there the sky; here the earth, there water; here a pylon, there a wire; here a canopy of trees, there the open air. Without lines, it is said, we would never be able to tell anything from anything else: the world would just be one big multi-coloured blur. But in her photographs,

Figure 23 Ploughed field, drainage ditch and wood.
(Photo by Nisha Keshav.)

Nisha Keshav proves, beyond doubt, that those who say that lines are but figures of thought, without any counterpart in the inhabited world, have got it completely wrong. There *are* lines in the landscape. Indeed these photographs offer vivid testimony to the fact that every living landscape is no more, and no less, than a composition of lines and elements.

Pencil a line on paper and look at it closely, under magnification. What is there but an elongated smudge of graphite, of varying width and density, ragged at the edges, and rubbed off from the pencil-point by the abrasions of the paper surface? Well, if this still counts as a line, then why not ruts left by tyres in the snow, why not the raked striations of a harrowed field, why not the groove of a drainage trench (Figure 23)? You can't have it both ways, allowing the pencil-mark on paper, but not the marks of toil and habitation in the land. Why should the meeting and mingling of graphite and paper, along your pencilled line, be any different in principle from the meeting and mingling of water with reed-banks along the length of the ditch? If the drawn line is formed from the friction of graphite on paper, are not the furrows of the field equally formed from the laborious drag of the rake or the plough against the resistance of the earth? If the former is a line, then the latter are lines too. Lines like this have a material presence; they are not just floating signifiers whose proper place lies in the domain of images. They are not metaphorical but real. And the most important thing about them is that they have not yet broken off from, or parted company with, the elements out of which they are formed – elements that include the crumpled earth, the turbulent air, precipitation and sunlight.

There are lines in the landscape because every landscape is forged in movement, and because this movement leaves material traces along the manifold paths of its proceeding. To perceive these lines is not to see things as they are but to see the directions along which things are moving. It is to see their grains, textures and flows, not their layout or their formal envelopes. We perceive the smudge of graphite on paper as a line because we see the way it is going, and it is no different with the furrow, the cloud and the reed. In every case, the line can be distinguished from its element, but not the element from the line. The pencil-mark is distinguished from the paper, but not paper from

Figure 24 Starlings on wires. (Photo by Nisha Keshav.)

mark; the furrow is distinguished from the earth, but not earth from furrow; the clouds from the sky, but not sky from clouds; the reeds from water-logged beds, but not beds from reeds. Observe again the striations of the field, carved by human labour, doused in rainwater and whipped by the wind under the luminous sky. These are lines of force and friction, and they criss-cross the landscape as the labours of agriculture intersect with running water, with the flights of birds and with the power cables on which the birds alight on their passage (Figure 24). Yes, there are lines in this landscape, and we have Nisha Keshav's photographs to prove it.

The chalk-line and the shadow

This essay, commissioned by arts director Benjamin Grillon, was origi-
nally written to accompany a photographic project by artists Matthieu
Raffard and Mathilde Roussel. The aim of the project was to explore
the relation between space, grid and line in the construction of images.
Raffard and Roussel were particularly interested in the chalk-line, a
simple tool still widely used in the construction industry for marking up
surfaces with straight lines. A line of string, coated in white or blue chalk,
is stretched tight across a surface. When plucked, it vibrates, immediately
marking the surface along its entire length. Is this line, traversing the
shortest distance between points, indifferent to surface obstruction, an
abstraction from the solid materials of the construction site? Or is it,
in its weight and tension, the material and tangible expression of the
notional, geometric lines of the architectural design? It is of course both,
a kind of pivot in the balance between conceptual and material worlds.
Therein lies its particular utility.

I am visiting the town of Hammerfest, on the coast of northern
Norway. It is a bright September day, and I am following a popular,
well-used path on the town's outskirts. Alongside one length of the
path the municipal authorities have erected a fence, consisting of
horizontal wires stretched between poles driven at intervals into the
ground. As I walk, I notice how the topmost wire of the fence casts
a shadow. To my astonishment, the shadow runs like a dark ribbon
directly along the midline of the path. Though the surface of the path
is itself somewhat irregular – a mixture of stone, mud and gravel,
worn down by countless feet – the ribbon passes effortlessly over
every obstruction, without once deviating from its course. Even more

remarkably, it vanishes instantaneously, along its entire visible length, the moment the sun goes behind a cloud – only to reappear, as if by magic, when the sun comes out again. I cannot help wondering about the strangeness of this line, and in particular about how it differs from the lines of the path itself and of the fence wire.

The thing about the path is that it continually makes itself out from the ground without ever parting company with it. Ask me how the path runs in the ground and I can tell you; ask me what is ground and what is path and I cannot. For the path is not laid *over* the ground surface but rather emerges as a differential *within* it, marked, for example, by additional wear and tear, the trampling of vegetation or erosion of the soil. In this regard, it is much like a line made by drawing. When you draw a line with a pencil on the page, the line emerges as the trace of the pencil-point moved by the gesture of your hand. With the path it is the movements of the feet, and not the hand, which leave a trace. Nevertheless, like the drawn line, the path is formed in the continuation of a bodily movement *as it goes along*. I am of course walking where many have gone before, and in that sense the line is already there for me to follow. Yet in following it I am contributing, however insignificantly, to its perpetuation.

With the wire, however, it appears to be quite otherwise. For far from being laid down by the wayfaring of feet or hands as they go along, the wire has been stretched between poles already driven into the ground. It is as though, in the stretched wire of the fence, the way of the path is broken down and reconstructed as a sequence of roughly equidistant points and the straight-line connections between them. The wire, moreover, cares nothing for the surface features of the ground over which it is suspended, as indeed the ground cares nothing for the wire. Walking the path, I have no difficulty in telling the one apart from the other.

Pausing for a moment, I look out to sea, and watch as a ship laden with liquefied natural gas from a nearby refinery plies the narrow channel separating the mainland from neighbouring islands. I imagine the ship's navigator, chart on screen, plotting a course from point to point. The lines on his chart, it seems to me, could have had no more business with the actual surface of the sea than the wire of the fence has with the surface of the ground. But if the line of navigation resembles the stretched wire in that respect, in another respect it could not be more different. For it exists only on screen, mapped onto a notional plane of cartographic representation. The wire, by contrast, has a real, substantive presence in the world. It has body, colour, texture. You can touch it and feel it. Pluck it, and it vibrates. In a strong wind, its vibrations can even generate a sound.

Let's go back to basics. This difference in the straight line, between abstract ideal and phenomenal presence, has been with us since the very origins of geometry. In Euclid's *Elements*, a straight line is minimally defined as the shortest distance between two points. As such, it is purely conceptual and rational. Infinitely thin, it is drawn upon a plane that is both transparent and without substance. Yet the first geometers – literally 'earth-measurers' – of whom we have certain knowledge were the surveyors of Ancient Egypt, who would stake out plots of land for cultivation after every annual flooding of the Nile, by stretching ropes between sticks driven into the ground. It is surely no accident that it was in Egyptian Antiquity, too, that we find the first evidence of a method for marking out stones prior to cutting, widely used by masons ever since. A thread, dusted in red ochre, would be stretched taut across the surface of the material to be cut. By plucking or snapping the thread, and causing it to vibrate, it would instantly leave a perfectly straight trace of ochre on the surface, which could then guide the hand of the cutter.

Now if the origin of the straight line lies in the taut thread, it is surely not unreasonable to suggest that the first straight lines to be traced on surfaces were snapped into place rather than drawn by hand. Nowadays, the preferred material is white or blue chalk, and the thread is commonly of nylon, wound on a reel, but the basic technique has otherwise remained unchanged (Figure 25). To mark a surface for cutting, on site, you unwind the thread from the reel, stretch it across the surface, and snap for the trace to appear.

As I walk, following the ribbon of shadow cast by the fence wire, I wonder whether the chalk-line might hold the clue to the relation

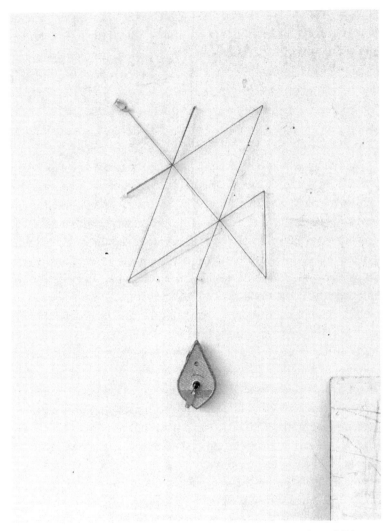

Figure 25 Chalk-line (2019), by Matthieu Raffard and Mathilde Roussel. (Photo courtesy of Benjamin Grillo Studio.)

between the wire and the ribbon. For it suddenly dawns on me that this relation is comparable to that between the chalk-line and its trace (Figure 26). They have in common that the force that activates the line, whether of chalk or wire, comes at it not longitudinally – as in

Figure 26 The shadow of the chalk-line (2019), by Matthieu Raffard and Mathilde Roussel. (Photo courtesy of Benjamin Grillo Studio.)

walking a path or drawing with a pencil – but transversally. As fingers pluck the thread, rays of sunlight strike across the wire, orthogonally to the line of tension. Both thread and wire, moreover, instantly cast a shadow, along their entire length. Seemingly floating over the roughness of the surface, indifferent to its variations, this shadow somehow blends with the surface without apparently touching it at all. And as the builder follows the shadow in cutting the material, I follow it with my feet in breaking the path.

There are differences, of course. For one thing, radiant sunlight cannot exactly pluck fence wire as the builder's finger plucks the string of his chalk-line, making it vibrate. And for another, while the shadow of the chalk-line remains as a material residue, long after the line has ceased vibrating, the shadow of the wire vanishes on the instant that the sun goes in. It is as insubstantial as a ghost. Touch such a shadow, and it will not smudge your hands. Nor, of course, can you wipe it out. Only a cloud can do that. But not all shadows are so ephemeral. On a photographic plate or blueprint, exposed to radiation, lines show up as indelible shadows cast upon the surface. But in contrast to the chalked thread, which deposits its pigment only on the line of contact with the surface, with the plate or print the entire surface is pigmented save the lines themselves. They are negatives. So is the dark ribbon of shadow on the otherwise illuminated path. The chalk-line, however, is positive.

With these thoughts weighing on my mind, I continue on my way. Out in the fjord, the ship steams out of sight, its wake trailing the line of the navigator. But for ever after during daylight hours, the ribbon will continue to vanish and reappear as the sun goes in and out, while bare earth is covered by snow, until – in the depth of the arctic winter – the sun itself is eclipsed in the shadow of the earth.

Fold

The geographical term for the line of lowest elevation formed where two slopes intersect, making a natural watercourse or pathway through the hills, is talweg *(literally the 'way of the dale'). In effect, the talweg is a fold in the landscape, and the river and the path follow it. No wonder that* TALWEG, *an artistic and literary review dedicated to reflections on the line, took 'fold' as the theme for its inaugural issue.[1] My contribution was a little poem that traces the meaning of the term, from the fold of the newspaper, through folding clothes and folded rock to the gathering of the flock. Folds are multiple. But like the fold-lines that crease the surfaces of the world, or that can be made out in a sheet of paper first crumpled and then spread out, they are variations of one.*

Fold
Where side by side is back to back or face to face.
What secrets lie between the sheets of bed or newspaper
Where words like bodies touch and kiss in unseen intimacy?
To read, the pages must be opened up,
And words that once had felt each other's pulse
Must stand apart as though they'd never known each other,
Divided by a crease.

Fold
Makes volumes out of surfaces
Packed up in drawers and suitcases,
Even as the smoothing iron makes surfaces from volumes.
The crumpled handkerchief and bulging pockets lie flat upon the
    board,

Figure 27 The meeting of letters across a fold.
(Photo by the author.)

The life pressed out of them. Clothes stacked neat upon the shelf,
Safe from sweaty pores and restless limbs,
Are only fit for shadows.

Fold
The very surface of the earth,
Bends and buckles when compressed by forces unimaginable.
To walk old mountains is to cross the ridges of a concertina,
Worn down by ages of erosion. Time itself loses its alignment, so
   that,
Much to the perplexity of geologists,
More ancient strata overtop their followers.

Fold
Two, four, many;
A thing that multiplies in growth and differentiation

Like a herdsman's flock or pastor's congregation.
Wanderings and ways of life gathered in church or pen,
Where they can be counted.
Multiplicity enfolded in a place, together, all-in-one.

Taking a thread for a walk

In a world of materials, there can be no lines without surfaces, no surfaces without lines. Wherever surfaces exist, they must have somehow formed through a linear weaving of materials. And wherever lines exist, they must either be traced in a surface or threaded through it. But as kinds of line, traces and threads have fundamentally different properties, and that is my theme in this essay. I wrote it after visiting the studio of the Brussels-based textile artists Anne Masson and Eric Chevalier.[1] Entering the studio, I found myself in a world where all the familiar things with which we surround ourselves in everyday life, such as clothes and furniture, are ravelling and unravelling, forming marvellous and unexpected patterns in the process. The lines had taken over. A ball of wool was becoming a vest, or was it the vest that was becoming a ball of wool? Chairs, their matted seats unravelling, were getting tangled up together, leaving us with nowhere to sit. Hooks meant to hang things on were hanging themselves on one another, with no regard for the things that should have hung on them.

Winding, tangling and hanging are things you can do with threads that you cannot do with traces. They can also be stretched, and plucked. And they can be cut. These are all afflictions of the flesh, itself a tissue of thread-lines. What happens, then, when flesh is wounded?

Of drawing, Paul Klee famously remarked that it is to take a line for a walk. Every drawn line is the trace of a gesture, a mark left on a surface by a moving point (see p. 86). But the trace is just one kind of line. Another kind, just as ubiquitous, is the thread. What would happen if we were to take a thread for a walk? There are some differences, to be sure. For one thing, unlike the trace, which simply

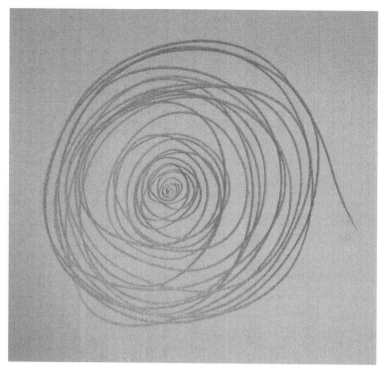

Figure 28 A wound-up pencil-line. (Photo by the author.)

extends as you go along, the thread has first to be spun. Even before you start your walk, the line must already have been prepared, and it will in all probability have been wound up, either in a ball or onto a spool. You can wind up a drawn line too, by a coiling movement of the pencil which is not unlike the movement of spooling a thread, as shown in Figure 28. What you cannot do with the trace, however, is unwind it; nor, having done so, can you wind it up again. Nor can you move it around or change its layout – though you can of course rub it out, which you cannot do with the thread.

For another thing, it is possible to stretch a thread. A stretched thread is straight and taut, like the string of a violin. Pluck or bow the string, and it vibrates. A trace cannot vibrate. Maybe it can record vibrations, as a seismograph, for example, registers the vibrations of the ground during an earthquake. But on the violin, it is the string itself that vibrates. Another example of the stretched thread is the warp of the loom. There are reasons to believe that the loom's warp-lines were the prototype for the ruled lines of the manuscript, leading to the parallel between the oscillations of the weft in weaving and of the letter-line in writing that still survives in the notion of writing as text.[2] But as practical operations, the stretching of a thread and the ruling of a line are quite different, for the former establishes a tension that the latter does not. The stretched line is energetic, the ruled line inert. The one owes its straightness to the play of forces intrinsic to the material and that have been imparted to it through the mechanics of spinning. The other's straightness is a mere reflex of the edge of the ruler that has been used as a jig to guide the movement of the marking point. If you stretch threads across a pliable surface, such as of card or even wood, the tension can be enough to warp the surface; no amount of ruling, however, will have the same effect. If the ruled lines are scored, then the likely result will be not to warp the surface laterally but to cut it longitudinally.

With these differences between trace and thread in mind, let us embark on our walk. We have a supply of thread – say, of wool – rolled up into a ball. This ball is an interesting thing in itself. You might compare it to the many kinds of balls designed to be rolled or hurled in games of various sorts. Gaming balls are discrete objects with continuous, spherical surfaces. When they make contact with other things – with the ground, with the hands or boots of players or with one another – it is through surface-to-surface impact. The ball of yarn, however, though spherical in form, has no coherent surface. In just the same way, the wound-up trace that I drew earlier (Figure 28) has no coherent perimeter. If you start looking for the surface of a ball of wool, you will end up unwinding it until nothing of the ball remains. Alternatively, if you have sufficient material in reserve, you could carry on winding. Would you, in so doing, cover up the ball's surface with a new layer? Not at all; for there was no surface to begin with. To put it another way, the ball of wool is never complete, it is always 'becoming ball', and the line of becoming is the thread. What holds it

Figure 29 Ball of wool, by Anne Masson and Eric Chevalier.
(Photo by Christian Aschman.)

all together is the tension in the thread, which makes it so that with every turn, one is in effect binding that which is bound so far. The ball is a binding, but it is a binding of nothing but itself (Figure 29). It can just as well be an unbinding, however, and that is precisely what happens when you begin to walk.

Taking your thread for a walk may require some tools. The most basic tool is the needle: a long, thin implement, pointed at one end, which may or may not be pierced by an eye at the other. In stitching and embroidery, the thread passes through the eye; in knitting, it is looped around the shaft. Either way, whether in sewing or knitting, the primary function of the tool is not to inscribe a trace, even though you could in principle use the sharp point to do just that. The tool does not make the line, for the line is already made. It rather does with the thread precisely what cannot be done with the trace – that is, to rearrange it into a pattern of loops or knots, where the purpose of the point is to find the opening, and that of the eye or shaft to pull through. Here, instead of spiralling on itself, as in the ball, the line forms an intricate tangle that can only be unravelled by undoing its loops. In the hands of the skilled sewer, the needle facilitates a kind of miniature acrobatics: on a larger scale it would be like a walk that proceeds not by putting one foot before the other but by a series of somersaults. Through regular repetition, the loops intertwine to form a fabric.

And so, on your acrobatic walk, the thread is re-bound into the fabric, as fast as it unwinds from the ball. The thread-line is neither ball nor fabric, nor is it something connecting the two as though ball and fabric were separate objects to be linked up. It is rather 'ball becoming fabric'. But it could just as well be 'fabric becoming ball'. The beauty of the thread is that what has once been ravelled can always be unravelled, only to be ravelled again so as to yield new and previously unanticipated forms and patterns (Figure 30). In both the ball and the fabric, however, there is a balance of tension and relaxation. This is why one can use such words as 'tight' or 'loose' to describe them, rather than the more conventional binary of 'closed' and 'open'. Cutting through a ball of yarn is almost like dissecting living flesh: the tension in the thread is immediately released on cutting, so that the two sides of the cut pull away to leave a gaping wound. Is there a connection between the winding of the ball and the flesh-wound? In a now obsolete sense, 'to wind' was indeed to wield a weapon in a curvy trajectory, designed to wound one's opponent. Living tissue, like the ball of wool, is a skein of thread-lines.

Similarly, cutting the threads of a fabric can generate patterned distortion, as the threads rearrange themselves to reach a new equilibrium, without any manual intervention on the part of the weaver. Rather like the exquisite patterns of bubbles that form in a dish of soapy water through the equilibration of forces of surface tension, so textile patterns express an equivalent equilibrium in the tensile forces of their constituent threads. And just as when you burst a bubble, so too when you cut a thread, the entire pattern is reconfigured. It arises, as we often say, 'of its own accord', though it would be more accurate to say that this accord is a kind of settlement arrived at

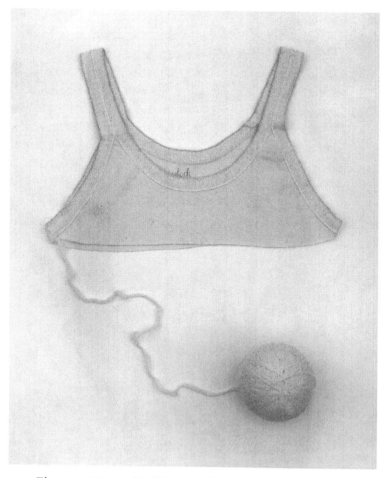

Figure 30 Vest and ball, by Anne Masson and Eric Chevalier.
(Photo by Christian Aschman.)

through a negotiation of forces among the cords – that is, the threads
– themselves.

Another word for accord might be sympathy. The concordant
threads of the textile are bonded in a sympathetic union. Like lines of
choral polyphony, but unlike the components of a sculptural assembly, they are bound not *up* but *with*. Indeed, with their alternations of
tension and resolution, their rhythmic structure, their counterpoints

and harmonies, textiles are much more akin to musical compositions than to works of sculpture. So when we see two chairs bound together, their objectness seems subordinated to their textility rather than the other way around. Originally, fresh from the shop or showroom, these chairs might have had matted seats; this woven element, however, would have been framed by the joined-up, carpentered assembly. But after many years of cohabitation they have developed a certain affinity, even love, framed within the mutual affections of their sitters. If the furniture we use every day is as much a part of us as the clothes we wear, then why can furniture not embrace as people do? Chairs, too, can love one another; though once they do, they might be of little use for sitting on (Figure 31). In such an upside-down world, it would

Figure 31 Two chairs in one, by Anne Masson and Eric Chevalier. (Photo by Christian Aschman.)

be the fate of humans to carry the weight of amorous furniture, and perhaps to withstand the pressures of discord as well, if and when amity turns to strife.

It is as if these ball-chairs were dancing the tango, with the same intimate intensity. No longer separate or separable objects, they are joined in a spherical embrace, two-in-one. To make a dance out of pieces of furniture is to show how they carry on their lives *with* us, as do we with them. Woven lives intermingle at their surfaces, which, like those of the ball of wool, do not cover up an interior world of private individuality so much as confound the layering of experience which such covering implies. Like the still water of a pond, in whose surface the reflected sky mingles with floating weed and refractions from the murky depths, the surface of fabric is a play of light and shadow, colour and tone, harmony and melody. The texture is a surface not of concealment or covering up but of intermingling. And it is on surfaces such as these that we walk our ever-extending threads of life.

Letter-line and strike-through

At the start of a brief video-work entitled Walk *(strike through with pen),*[1] *the artist Anna Macdonald is filmed seated on a stool in the middle of a field (Figure 32(a)). She is holding a sheaf of papers, which flutter in the breeze. The field itself is nondescript: flat, a bit muddy, mixed with scraggly grass and weeds. The horizon is cluttered with leafless trees, and the sky devoid of features. It must be late autumn or winter. There is some distant birdsong, but no other sound apart from a slightly ominous hissing or grating that ends with a little click, as though a pen were being pulled from its holder. Quietly, deliberately, Macdonald rises from her stool and, looking straight ahead, begins to walk. On screen we see her figure in profile, as it proceeds from left to right. After only a few paces, however, there is a sudden slashing sound, and a brown-black line streaks across the frame, cutting through the figure of the walking artist just below her neck (Figure 32(b)). With barely a moment's hesitation, she carries on, and the line soon fades, only for the same thing to happen again, this time cutting her figure at the level of the waist (Figure 32(c)). After some twenty paces, she stops and turns about to face the stool. There is another slash, now cutting through her face (Figure 32(d)). The video ends, after just a minute and eighteen seconds, with the picture fading, leaving only the line of the slash. Attending to the background, we realize that the mark was actually made on the textured surface of paper, and that the video-image, too, had played upon the same surface. What is going on here?*

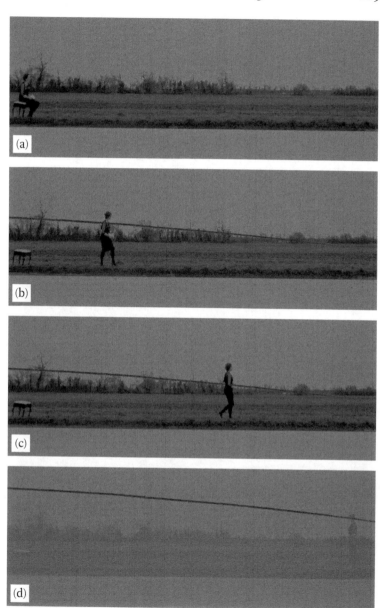

Figure 32 Four stills from *Walk (strike through with pen)* (2016) by Anna Macdonald: (a) at 0' 03"; (b) at 0' 30"; (c) at 0' 39"; (d) at 1' 10".
(Courtesy of the artist.)

In a world of life, lines grow from the tip. Roots and runners, feeling their way through the soil, twist and turn in response to ever-varying conditions. Shoots and saplings flex as they compete to find their place in the sun. On land, animals track erratically through the undergrowth, while birds flit from branch to branch, or soar on winding currents of air. On a busy street, people weave in and out to avoid collision. And in the simple act of writing with a pen, fingertip gestures of the thinking hand leave a wiggly trace in the form of the letter-line. In most occidental writing systems, the line goes from left to right. But the pen makes only slow progress from one margin of the page to the other. Much of the time it is oscillating up and down, or even looping back before issuing forth again.

The strike-through, however, is another matter altogether. It is sudden, violent and explosive. The axe, striking through timber, cleaves it in twain; the swords of warriors, striking through flesh, leave the battlefield strewn with severed limbs; heads roll from under the guillotine. And a canvas, slashed by the vandal's knife, is left with a gaping tear. In every case, the cutting edge is propelled like a projectile, under its own momentum. When it comes to cutting cloth, our implement of choice might rather be a pair of scissors: slicing the material as they close, scissor-blades sever the threads of which the material was once woven with twice the force of the single-bladed knife. And in taking scissors to paper, their blades likewise cut through text as through the threads of fabric, reducing it to shreds.

Fortunately, however, striking through text with a pen has no such dire consequences. The gesture is similar. It is equally impulsive. The hand swings into action, and proceeds without hesitation or deviation. The arc-like trace it leaves, unless guided by a ruler, resembles more the trajectory of a missile than the root's meander or pedestrian's walk. Yet whatever lies beneath the trace remains intact. If it is an image, such as on a picture postcard, it can still be seen; if it is text, as on the reverse of the card, it can still be read. To be sure, the intruding line can get in the way, making both viewing and reading a little more difficult. But compared to the alternatives, of slicing or shredding, on the one hand, or scratching or rubbing out, on the other, the inscriptive strike-through uniquely preserves its deletions, and may even enhance their significance. As the artist Jean-Michel Basquiat admits: 'I cross out words so you will see them more; the fact that they are obscured makes you want to read them.'[2] Indeed it takes only a slight downward shift to convert the cross-out into an underline, turning deletion into emphasis. The question is: how is this possible?

Philosophers from Martin Heidegger to Jacques Derrida have made much of the idea of writing 'under erasure' (in French, *sous rature*), as a way of having your cake and eating it so far as words are concerned.[3] The words are never quite right, so you want to cross them out, yet you cannot do without them, so you make sure they remain legible. Strictly speaking, however, to erase a word is to render it functionally *illegible*. Unlike crossing out, it is a surface-oriented movement that scrapes off a top layer, including whatever text or imagery might be inscribed into it. Most often, removal is only partial, with the result that reuse leads to the formation of a palimpsest. But in the palimpsest, as we saw on p. 88, erasure brings old words to the surface, rather than putting them, as it were, behind bars. Only a philosopher could confuse, under the same idea, practical operations so different, in both enactment and effect, as rubbing out and crossing out! No scribe, typesetter or proof-reader would make the same mistake. Nor would they mistake either rubbing or crossing, both of which preserve the integrity of the surface, for slicing or shredding, which destroys it. While fragments might survive the shredder, they have to be reassembled to be read, much as an archaeologist might piece together the sherds of an ancient pot to recover its form and decoration, or as a prospective fraudster might hope to reconstruct the details of a credit card from the cut-up shreds of paper receipts.

What is so distinctive about the strike-through with a pen, compared with the cleave of the cutter, is that the gesture, along with the trace it leaves, unfolds on a separate plane of reality, one that is layered over the original without ever making contact with it. To explain what I mean, let me turn to a very different example. Measuring 29.5 inches tall by 28.5 inches wide, John James Audubon's *Birds of America* is one of the largest books ever printed.[4] Every page is graced with a portrait of a particular bird, native to the continent, and the book owes its size principally to Audubon's determination to paint each species in its actual life size. The book was to be the two-dimensional equivalent of the taxidermist's three-dimensional diorama, and as with the diorama, each portrait was placed in a model landscape appropriate to its kind. Figure 33 reproduces Audubon's portrait of the whooping crane. You see how the bird's neck is bent over, into an anatomically impossible conformation, in order to fit on the page. But you can also see that its beak is open, apparently poised to snap up a lizard basking on the ground. Look again, however, and you realize that the bird and the lizard belong to two quite different pictures. The lizard is part of a painting of a landscape which includes ground, forest and a lake. The bird, depicted on a quite different scale, has been pasted onto this background, much as you might paste a picture onto wallpaper. And while the bird, like the taxidermist's model, feigns a certain reality, the landscape is manifestly a representation, as if reflected in a looking glass. The bird, then, can no more strike the lizard than it can go behind the glass.

We can now return to Anna Macdonald's video, reassured in the knowledge that the pen, streaking three times across the width of the frame, can do no more harm to her walking body than can the crane's beak to the crouching lizard. In fact, pen and body make no contact at all, and the illusion that they do is no more than an artefact of superposition. When you strike through timber with an axe, you-with-your-axe and the timber are co-participants in the same world. With one strike of the axe, the timber is rent asunder. But in the video, two separate worlds are juxtaposed: the outdoor world of field and woods and the indoor world of pen and paper. Indeed, in the making of the piece, the pen-line's streak across the paper was separately filmed and layered over an earlier film of the artist's field-walking. The sounds were similarly superimposed, as the hiss of the pen's retraction from its holder plays over birdsong. At the start of the video, we are so much immersed in the outdoor world, behind the looking glass, that

Figure 33 *Whooping Crane*, from *Birds of America* (1827–38), by John James Audubon. (Courtesy of the John James Audubon Center, Mill Grove, Pennsylvania.)

we sense the abrupt appearance of the strike-through as an alien intrusion, which soon fades. 'What on earth was that?' we wonder. But by the end, we are back before the glass, in the world of pen and paper, while the image of the artist in the field fades like a dream on waking.

What does all this tell us, then, about the strike-through of verbal inscription? When we correct ourselves in writing, or edit text, we simply and routinely strike through the words to be deleted. Yet in truth, the strike-through crosses over the letter-line *without ever touching it*. The letter-line can loop around itself, like a yarn in knitting. Other lines can be inserted or woven into the text. The one thing the letter-line cannot do, however, is reel back and cross itself out. Nor, for that matter, can it underline itself. Paradoxically, the strike-through, although inscribed on the same page as the letter-line it appears to delete, belongs to an entirely separate register of inscription. Indeed it makes no more contact with the text than does the underline. Shifting the altitude of the strike up or down, for example from ~~erasure~~ to erasure,[5] affects its significance, but does not change the register. You could compare it to looking through a window divided into panes. The horizontal transom that divides the upper from the lower panes bisects your view of the outdoors, crossing over a certain feature of interest. You want to see the feature more clearly? To do so, you need only raise your sights a little, whereupon the transom line dips to a level beneath the feature in question, putting it more prominently in the frame. Yet the transom, of course, belongs to the window, and not to the world outside.

It is the same with the strike-through and the letter-line, and their intersection likewise epitomizes the condition of the writer, whose imagination roams heaven and earth, mingling with the soil, wind and birdsong of the outdoor world, yet whose hand – confined to the indoor world of the study – is locked into a myopic engagement with the page. In the strike, these worlds accidentally collide, and the trace it leaves is the mark of their collision.

FOR THE LOVE OF WORDS

Introduction

For most of us, as we go about our lives, words furnish our principal means of correspondence. With them, we invite others to gather round, converse with them, join our own life-stories with theirs, attend and respond to what they say and do. Enriched by the patina of everyday use, ever-varying in texture, they rise up in the gestures of the mouth and lips in speech, or spill out onto the page in the traces of the writer's hand. They can be noisy or quiet, turbulent or serene. Words, spoken or handwritten, echo to the pulse of things. They can caress, startle, enchant, repel. As the philosopher Maurice Merleau-Ponty once put it, they are so many ways we have of singing the world and its praises.[1] We could say that words mediate a poetics of habitation.

Yet looking around, it seems that something has gone seriously wrong in our relations with words. It is as though they have turned against us, or we against them. We routinely hold them to blame for the suppression of feeling, or for failing to account for the authenticity of experience. To get to what it really feels like, we insist, we have to get beneath the words, or behind them. Words, it seems, are no longer our habit or our dress. Rather, they have become the means by which we dress things up, coating them with a gloss that obscures the truth these things might tell if left to be themselves. Of course there are still people who use words to plumb the depths of human feeling. But they have become the purveyors of a specialist – and, for many, an arcane – craft. Instead of inhabiting the world poetically, we have created a little niche in the inhabited world for poets.

Perhaps no contemporary community has developed a greater antipathy towards words than that which principally works with them. I mean the community of scholars, and, above all, those scholars who would regard themselves as academics. Scholars are people who study; academic scholars, however, think of study in a particular way. For far from studying *with* the world, or allowing themselves to be taught by it, they make studies *of* the world, claiming in so doing to have reached heights of intellectual superiority from which things are revealed with a clarity and a definition denied to ordinary folk. This sovereign perspective requires of academics to keep their distance from the matters of their concern, and not to get their hands dirty by mingling with them. Above all, they must ensure their words are sterile. Like the instruments of the surgeon, they should not be stained by visceral contact, whether with their operators or with that on which they operate. Words are to be utilized – but not used – to signify but not to mean, to articulate but not to say, to explicate but not to tell.

Using, meaning, saying and telling are ways we have of bringing others close, of drawing them into our life and custom. But to utilize, signify, articulate or explicate is to hold them at arm's length, abjuring contact. It is to maintain at least a semblance of objectivity. Yet objectivity stops us in our tracks, forbidding us from allowing things or persons into our presence, so that we might answer to them. It blocks correspondence. If we are really to study *with* the world, then this block must be removed. And if we are to do it with words, then words – and particularly written words – must be liberated from the *cordon sanitaire* the academy has thrown around them. In the four brief pieces that follow, I call for the restoration of words to the hand, to the movement of their production, and to the feeling that such movement calls forth. Perhaps, then, they can at last escape the quarantine of academia and make it back into the fullness of human life.

Words to meet the world

The traditional academic settlement places words on the near side, and the world on the far side, of an impregnable ontological barrier. It seems that words and world can never meet. As a scholar and an academic myself, I have long resented this division. I am by no means alone in this, however. The last several years have seen numerous experiments with alternative ways of writing that would restore the voices of scholarship to participation in the world of which they speak. Some of these experiments were recently assembled into a volume of essays on the theme of non-representational methods, edited by ethnographer and film-maker Philip Vannini.[1] Not one of the contributors to the collection, however, went so far as to toy with alternatives to the keyboard and screen, in the act of writing itself. In this piece, originally written as the foreword to the volume, I reflect on the possibility of doing just this.

One night, a few years ago, I woke from a dream with the following lines in my head:

> Often in the midst of my endeavours,
> Something ups and says,
> 'Enough of words.
> Let's meet the world.'

I do not know who put these lines there. Certainly, I did not invent them. But immediately upon waking, and before they had time to evaporate, I rose from my bed to write them down. They remain, pinned to a notice-board in my study, and every so often I take a look at them, to remind myself of the message they contain.

They could perhaps be taken as a manifesto for a way of working that abhors representation. This is not exactly a theory, nor is it a method or technique as this is commonly understood. It is not a set of regulated steps to be taken towards the realization of some predetermined end. It is a means, rather, of carrying on and of being carried, that is, of living a life with others – humans and non-humans all – that is cognizant of the past, finely attuned to the conditions of the present and speculatively open to the possibilities of the future. This is what I have been calling *correspondence*, in the sense not of coming up with some exact match or simulacrum for what we find in the things and happenings going on around us, but of *answering* to them with interventions, questions and responses of our own. It is as though we were involved in an exchange of letters. 'Let's meet the world', for me, is an invitation – an exhortation or command even – to join in such a correspondence. It is, at the same time, a complaint against the cowardice of scholars who would preferably retreat into a stance that I once heard described as 'tangentialism', in which our meeting is but a glance that sheers away from the uncomfortable business of mixing our own endeavours too closely with the lives and times of those with whom our studies have brought us into contact. Indeed, correspondence and tangentialism are precise opposites, and they entail quite different understandings of what is meant by scholarship.

'Enough of words', my muse declared, and I sympathize. We are suffering, especially in academic life, from a surfeit of words. It would not be so bad if these words, like good food, were rich in flavour, varied in texture and left a lingering taste in the contemplative feelings they evoke. Carefully selected and well-prepared words are conducive to rumination. They enliven the spirit, which responds in kind. But the fact that most word-craft of this kind has been hived off to a restricted domain, known as poetry, is indicative of where the problem lies. If writing had not lost its soul, then what need would we have of poetry? We go there to find what otherwise is lost. Relentlessly bombarded by the formulaic confections of academic prose, weighed down with arcane vocabulary, honorific name-calling and ever-extending lists of citations, my muse had had enough. So have I. But I would not want to go the whole way, and to give up on words altogether. Words are, indeed, our most precious possessions and should be treated as such, like a casket of sparkling jewels. To hold such jewels is to cup the world in the palm of your hand. We *can* correspond with words, as letter-writers used to do, but only if we allow our words to shine.

The challenge, then, is to find a different way of writing. We have to experiment: to try things out and see what happens. To date, however, our experiments have been constrained by the conventions of the printed word. These conventions make writing seem like an act of verbal composition, rather than one of inscriptive performance. With a keyboard wired up to a mechanical printer – the typical apparatus of the academic writer – the expressive possibilities of the word, as a succession of marks on paper, are sorely limited. To be sure, one can vary the font, and use various means of highlighting, but these are nothing compared with the continuous modulations of feeling and form in a simple calligraphic line – a line that registers every nuance of the hand that draws it. If our words are truly to shine like jewels, must they not be restored to the hand?

Surely, our reflections on ways of working cannot be confined to matters of style and composition. They must also extend to the instruments we use, and their orchestration. How does the keyboard compare with the pen, pencil and brush? Let's try them out and see. Perhaps, then, we will find that working with words, the writer can once again become a draughtsman or an artist, or even a musician of sorts. We might cease our endless writing *about* performance, and become performers ourselves. The art of correspondence demands no less. It could be because of our addiction to the keyboard that we academics are so taken with the idea of tacit, embodied knowledge. We think, like my muse, that the only way to join with the world – that is, to participate in its unfolding from the very inside of our being – is by escape from the domain of the word, of representation. It seems to us that words are always on the outside: they articulate, specify, make explicit. As such, their role is to pin things down, to define them and render them immobile.

Yet behind these tapped-out words of ours, the beating heart of the tacit continues to animate our movements and feelings, and to show its hand in voice and gesture. Why, then, should this voice and gesture be wordless? Only because we start from a notion of the word from which all traces of vocal and manual performance, of expression and affect, have been stripped away. This is the kind of word we academics are used to, and it puts us in league with the professions for which an academic training is deemed essential: statesmen, bureaucrats, lawyers, doctors and managers. But this is not the word of poets, singers, actors, calligraphers and craftsmen. For them, the word is performed, often noisily and turbulently, in skilled and sensuous bodily practice – not just in the practice of handwriting, signing, singing or speaking, but in reading aloud. If this is the domain of the tacit, then the tacit is neither wordless nor silent. It is raucously verbal. It is in the realm of the explicit, not the tacit, that silence reigns. Here alone, adrift upon the printed page, the word has lost its voice. Tacit is to explicit as voiced to voiceless, not the other way around.

Perhaps, then, we need a new understanding of language, one that brings it back to life as a practice of 'languaging'. In a living language – one that is not semantically locked into a categorical frame but endlessly creating itself in the inventive telling of its speakers – words can be as lively and mobile as the practices to which they correspond. They can be exclamatory, as when the practitioner cries out with the satisfaction of a job well done, inviting others to join in its appreciation, or, alternatively, when things go off course, leading to error and mishap. And they can be discursive, as in their use in narrative and storytelling. But in neither case are they joined up, or articulated, in explicit, propositional forms. Does that make them any less verbal? Who, other than those whose lives are confined to the academy, would be so pompous, and so limited in their imaginative horizons, as invariably to put the word 'articulate' before the word 'speech' or 'writing', in such a way as to relegate to the sub-linguistic or non-verbal any utterance or inscription that is not syntactically structured as a joined-up assembly? In truth, it is articulation that has silenced the word, by drawing it out and fixing its co-ordinates of reference, independently of the vocal-gestural currents of its production.

Let's not be afraid, then, to meet the world with words. Other creatures do it differently, but verbal intercourse has always been our human way, and our entitlement. But let these be words of greeting, not of confrontation; of questioning, not of interrogation or interview; of response, not of representation; of anticipation, not of prediction. This is not to say that we should all become poets or novelists, let alone that we should seek to emulate philosophers, who, when it comes to their worldly involvements, have signally failed to practise what they preach, and for whom neither coherence of thought nor clarity of expression has ever been among their strongest suits. But it does mean that we should work our words as craftsmen work their materials, in ways that testify, in their inscriptive traces, to the labour of their production, and that offer these inscriptions as things of beauty in themselves.

In defence of handwriting

This piece once again recommends the restoration of writing to the hand. I wrote it for a series entitled Writing Across Boundaries, *hosted online by the Department of Anthropology at Durham University, for which a number of academic writers in the humanities and social sciences were invited to reflect on their practice.[1] I was one of them.*

I used normally to write by hand, with a fountain pen. In the past I would never use a typewriter unless I had to, and I must have been among the last to succumb to the temptations of the word processor. The very idea that writing involved a processing of words appalled me. Today, however, I catch myself tapping more and more on the keys of my laptop, with only occasional recourse to the pen. I find this both worrying and frustrating. I know I am doing it only because, like most academics, I am pressed for time. The computer is nothing more, and nothing less, than a box of short-cuts. Admittedly, some are handy. When, for example, I am trying to get the sentences of a paragraph in a sensible order, it helps to be able to try out different permutations until the solution eventually falls out. Other short-cuts merely facilitate the correction of errors that arise from the technology itself. I rarely make spelling mistakes when I write by hand, but do so frequently when I type. This is in part because my clumsy and untrained fingers keep hitting the wrong keys. More importantly, however, it is because my hand knows words as continuous, flowing gestures and not as sequences of discrete letters.

In a cursive script, the line, as it unravels upon the page, issues directly from this gestural movement, with all the care, feeling and devotion that goes into it. I compare it to practising my cello. When I practise – which I do as often as I can – the sound pours out from the contact between bow and strings. In just the same way, handwriting flows from the moving point of contact between pen and paper. The keyboard ruptures this connection. The tapping of my fingers on the keys bears no relation to the marks that appear on the page or screen. These marks carry no trace of movement or feeling. They are cold and expressionless. Typing on the computer, I find, is joyless and soul-destroying. It rips the heart out of writing.

I am saddened by the rule, observed in my own institution as in most others, that requires students to produce work in a standardized, word-processed format. I am told that one reason for this rule is that it allows work to be checked for originality, using anti-plagiarism software. From the start, students are introduced to the idea that academic writing is a game whose primary object is to generate novelty through the juxtaposition and recombination of materials from prescribed sources. Word processors were expressly designed as devices with which to play this game, and it is one in which many academics, having been trained in its conventions, are only too keen to indulge. But the game is a travesty of the writer's craft. Contrary to university regulations, I encourage my students to write by hand, as well as to draw, and to compare their experience of doing so with that of using the computer. The response has been unequivocal. Handwriting and drawing, they report, re-awaken long-suppressed sensibilities and induce a greater sense of personal involvement, leading in turn to profound insight.

Colluding in a culture of expectation that values novelty over profundity, and product over process, institutions have got their priorities back to front. There is nothing intrinsically wrong with copying stuff out. As musicians and calligraphers have always known, whether practising a piece or writing out a text, copying is a form of meditation that can slowly but assuredly lead to deep understanding. It involves the practitioner's entire being: the hand that writes or plays the work, the mind that dwells on its meaning, and the memory that fixes it. Thus the problem lies not in copying *per se*, but in the possibility that the computer affords to short-cut the laborious processes of rewriting and redrafting by the mere touch of a button. As copying *is* thinking, to short-cut copying is to bypass thought itself. By its nature, thinking twists and turns, drifts and meanders. A hunter who followed a bee-line from a point of departure to a predetermined destination would never catch prey. To hunt you have to be alert for clues and ready to follow trails wherever they may lead. Thoughtful writers need to be good hunters.

Yet thinking is not confined to moments while you hold a pen, let alone to periods spent staring at the computer screen. It is continuously on the go, and at any time of day and night it can unexpectedly congeal into a revelation that catches the essence of what you have been trying to say. You have to be ready to write it down, for it can otherwise pass as quickly as a dream on waking. Many writers keep a hardback notebook with them at all times precisely for such eventualities. I do too.

I would like to conclude, however, with a word in praise of breakfast cereal. Sheets of card cut from used cereal packets are perfect for catching thoughts on the fly. They are sufficiently stiff that you do not need anything to press on, and large enough to allow ample, unruled space. Sometimes I wake up in the early morning with a problem paragraph that I had been struggling with for all of the previous day now perfectly formed in my head. Propped up in bed, I quickly write it down on a cereal packet card. I can write a few hundred words in barely a tenth of that number of minutes, and having done so, and with the words securely saved, I can then move on. Many of the passages I am most proud of started life in this way. I have never come across anything that works quite as well as cereal packets. They beat the computer hands down. Try it, and you'll see!

Diabolism and logophilia

This piece was originally written as a foreword to a collection of essays by the historical geographer Kenneth R. Olwig.[1] *For decades, Olwig has championed a humanistic understanding of the idea of landscape, urging us to acknowledge its roots in agrarian practices that long predated its theatricalization, as stage and scenery, in the early modern period. In Olwig's work, moreover, this focus on landscape has always been accompanied by a fascination with words and their etymology. For him, the histories of land use and word use are so closely entwined as to be virtually inseparable. To cherish the landscape in which we dwell, it is imperative that we also cherish the words with which we speak and write.*

I switched on the radio early this morning to hear a programme devoted to farming. There was a feature on growing and harvesting seed potatoes, and a farmer who had made this his business was explaining the importance of maintaining purity in the seed stock, of which all the potatoes that reach our tables are essentially clones. 'We have to keep an eye out,' he said, 'for UDVs.' 'UDVs?' queried the presenter. 'Yes,' came the reply, 'that's *undesirable variants.*' It struck me that the farmer's response was truly *diabolical.* This is a word that takes pride of place in the collected essays of Kenneth Olwig. Ostensibly devoted to the long and thorny history of the idea of landscape, these essays speak to much wider issues of the fate of humanity – and, by extension, of the humanities, of language, letters and learning – in a world apparently caught in a diabolic spiral of contempt for the word, and consequent dehumanization, and in which the utopian dream of total techno-scientific control is turning more and more lives inside out. In this brave new world, at once universal but nevertheless reserved for those of appropriate breeding, people previously used to living together in difference are cast out, like the farmer's potatoes, as UDVs. Branded as migrants, refugees or stateless persons, they are displaced from home only to find themselves unwelcome abroad.

Words are human things. They are the ways we have of making our presence felt, while also bringing into presence the persons, places and matters – that is, the *topics* – whereof we speak. With words we call these topics to mind, dwell on them and join with others who do likewise, be it in friendship or hostility, commonality or difference, agreement or dispute. UDV, however, is not a word but an acronym. And if words are ways of joining with the world, acronyms serve the opposite end, of cutting us off. With the acronym we can identify the matters of our concern while at the same time turning our backs on them, abstaining from the involvement that would come from speaking their names. By identifying non-standard potatoes as UDVs, the farmer can stand back, neither giving voice to his desire, nor owning up to the skilled attentiveness that alerts him to variation. He can feign detachment, indifference and objectivity. The acronym repudiates presence, puts matters out of mind and banishes affect. But at the same time it betokens an authority based not on skill and attention but on allegedly objective principles of rational management. Thus the acronym is an instrument of oversight in both its senses: it overlooks and yet looks over, declines to attend to its referents while subjecting them to audit and control. It is no wonder that the colonization of language by acronyms has grown in proportion to the advance of science and technology, both backing and backed by the power of corporations and the state.

Nowhere is this more evident than in the field of military operations. The UK Ministry of Defence has published a list of some 20,000 acronyms, among them the well-known IED ('improvised explosive device'), WMD ('weapon of mass destruction') and SAM ('surface-to-air missile'), but also including the more sinister HK and SK ('hard kill' and 'soft kill'). Some, such as NKZ ('nuclear killing zone'), present the literally unspeakable as simple matters of fact.[2]

The violence the acronym does to language, here, parallels the violence that militarization does to the land. It was, after all, the military that brought mapping and survey to the British Isles under the guise of ordnance, the artillery of war. Where the acronym reduces words to markers of identification, the cartographic map reduces places to locations in space. And if the acronym enables the military commander to speak the unspeakable, the map enables him to plan destruction on an unimaginable scale, while remaining indifferent to its human consequences. Both are diabolical for the same reason. As Olwig explains, the prefix *dia-* has its etymological source in the classical Greek for 'crossover', while *bolos* connotes a 'throw'. The diabolical, then, is a throwing across, in which map and territory, language and world, having once been divided from one another, are conflated such that the territory becomes its own map, and the map its own territory. It is this diabolism that enables the military to treat the substantive landscape as a gaming board, and its inhabitants as pawns whose misfortune it may be to occupy a location targeted by a SAM, or a space marked on the map as an NKZ.

The fortunes of landscape and language are indissolubly bound, and in the current day and age, they are equally under attack. For techno-science, words are a distraction. They get in the way, and cloud our perception. Words routinely stand accused of hiding the objective truth of things, of falsifying reality, of covering up the facts. And place attachments, for their part, are seen to stand in the way of resource extraction, global markets and international development. The contemporary world, we might say, is not just *logophobic* but *topophobic*. Olwig's essays, to the contrary, set out to celebrate both word and place. Indeed their author is an unashamed *logophile*. He always has a dictionary to hand, and will leap at any excuse to consult it. For him, it is a leap not out of reality but directly into it, revealing the evolution of a lifeworld in all its richness, diversity and temporal depth. And this *logophilia* leads, in turn, to what Olwig's erstwhile mentor – the great humanistic geographer Yi-Fu Tuan – called *topophilia*: the affective bond between people and place.[3] This is not because words stand for places, or substitute for them. It is because words *make* places, in their very vocal and written performance. They make them in law, in custom, in the telling of stories, in the everyday conversation of neighbours, and in their coming together to deliberate on affairs in common. And the making of places, and of things as places of assembly, is also the making of the landscape – literally land that is continually shaped in the processes of human fellowship.

It is in this coming together, Olwig argues, that language and landscape are rendered symbolic. Once more, he takes us on an etymological excursion, to the origins of the term in the combination of the prefix *sym-*, from the Greek for going along together, with the 'throw' of *bolos*. In this original sense, of 'throwing together', of fellowship in a shared conversation or lifeworld, the symbolic stands as the very opposite of the diabolic. Where the diabolic, having divided the strategic space of cartographic representation from its territorial foundation, cuts across and conflates the two, the symbolic takes up the stories of concurrent lives and weaves them together in their ongoing and mutually responsive co-generation. The lesson we learn from Olwig's essays is that to avoid the diabolical scenario of total technocratic control, in a world purged of UDVs, we should turn not to objective facts but to real things. These are the assemblies of discourse and wisdom, of desire and variation, which have long comprised the soil of human flourishing. It behoves us to attend to them. And to achieve this, the first step must be to overcome the *logophobia* that afflicts the modern mind, and that has so infected our language as to collapse its idioms into mechanical key-strokes and acronymic character-strings. We must fall back in love with words. And as love turns to study, so should the logophile become a philologue. Philology, relegated by techno-science to the margins of scholarship, as the dusty hobby of antiquarians, should once again take centre-stage. In it lies nothing less that the future of scholarship, and of our common humanity.

Cold blue steel

Everyone has a different way of holding a pen, and of writing with it, just as everyone has a different voice. For each of us, our handwriting is inseparable from who we are. Yet in our digital age, it is increasingly despised. As verbal traffic has accelerated, words have become more and more detached from the lives and feelings of pressured writers, who are quick to fire them off rather than to pour their passion into them. How can we recover the melodic beauty of the written word as it takes shape under the hand? How can an action so ephemeral be turned into something lasting, something we can admire and celebrate? How can the exchange of words become, once again, a meeting of the hands and hearts that wrote them? These questions are central to the work of the Scottish artist Shauna McMullan. In an installation entitled Something About a Word, *McMullan invited a hundred people from Bridgeton, a district on the east side of Glasgow, to contribute – in their own handwriting – with thoughts inspired by the colour blue. I wrote this essay in response to a request from the artist to reflect on the work for an accompanying booklet.[1] It led me to think again about what happens to words when what begin as gestural traces are solidified into objects.*

For some time, I have been carrying around a very peculiar object in my pencil-case. There it is, jostling with assorted pens and pencils, ruler, rubbers, pencil-sharpener and paper-clips (Figure 34). I show it to people and ask them whether they can tell me what it is. None has any idea. The object is, in fact, a word. Now words are not usually the kinds of things you would carry in a pencil-case. The case is for the tools you need to make words, not for the words themselves. Of course we carry words around with us as well; they are in our heads,

Figure 34 The contents of my pencil-case. (Photo by the author.)

in memory and on paper, between the covers of pocket books. Yet, surely, if a word is to be held and carried rather than uttered – if it is to be a thing we take with us, care for and cherish rather than allow to escape our lips into oblivion – then it must be traced, inscribed or embroidered into some surface or other, whether neural or material. But my word is not graven in my memory, emblazoned on my clothing or scribbled on a slip of paper that I keep in my pocket lest I forget. Nevertheless, wherever I go, my word comes with me. How is this possible? And why can no-one else recognize the word for what it is?

Here's how, and why. The word had indeed first been written on paper, in a cursive and somewhat hurried hand. If there is anything out of the ordinary about this hand, it is that the writer had based the letter forms on Roman capitals, which had been contrived to run into one another along a single line so that the whole word could still be written without raising the pen. This required some bending and stretching of forms classically designed to stand alone or side by side and to be chiselled into solid stone. The next step was to scan the handwritten word and to feed the scan into a machine capable of cutting mild steel, six millimetres thick, with pin-point precision. The result is a rigid, hard and weighty three-dimensional object, having the form of a strip of constant width and thickness, but with bends, loops and protrusions corresponding exactly to those of the original script. The line of ink has become a ribbon of steel. I can pick the word up or set it down, hold it between my fingers and feel the edges of the letter-line, examine it from front and back and every possible angle, and even wave it about while grasping it from one end or the other! These are not things you can do with words on paper.

Yet this freedom, it seems, comes at a cost. For without your knowing what I have just told, you would be unable to read my word, or even to recognize it as a word at all. It would appear, as to everyone to whom I have shown it, simply as a mystery object, an enigma. This cannot be just because it is cast in three dimensions. After all, we urban dwellers are quite used to seeing solid letters, often on a grand scale and even illuminated, attached to shop fronts and in signage, and we have no trouble in recognizing them and in spelling out the words they compose. What is striking about these urban letters, however, is that they are for the most part passive and immobile, and bear not the slightest trace of the processes that went into their formation. Most often they are capitals. From infancy, we are taught to recognize capitals by their shapes, not by the movements by which they are formed. Even before they can read, we give children capital letters cut from wood or moulded from plastic to play with. Through this early training, we encourage them to think of words as assemblies built up from blocks rather than compositions of movement and gesture.

Indeed in the passivity and immobility of block capitals – that is, in their monumentality – lies the very source of their power and authority. They rule over us as the state over its citizens, and are there to stifle or stamp out any traces of voice, feeling and affect. They remind us of the caustic conclusion of Claude Lévi-Strauss, namely that the true purpose for which writing was invented was to facilitate slavery.[2] Yet the writer of my word has cleverly subverted the authority of capitals by co-opting them into the practice of a cursive script. In this, the monument has been put to everyday use and its pretensions to power are laid bare. The once rigid letters bend and stretch; they become part of a movement. When we write by hand, we remember letters and words as movements, as gestures, not as shapes. Moreover, these gestures, which both are inspired by and carry forth our feelings, moods and motivations, translate directly and without interruption into the lines on the page. In this regard, the pen of the handwriter is like the bow of the string-player: the writer's line, like the player's, is at once dynamic, rhythmic and melodic. And if it is by movement that the line is laid, so it is by movement, too, that we read it.

To read handwriting on paper, however, is to follow the trace left behind by a hand that has already moved on. We can pick up the trail, but the impulse that created it is spent. We always arrive a little too late. Cut in steel, however, it is as though the word were preserved in the very moment of its formation, like an insect caught in amber. The force of the word, the energy of the writer's hand and the feeling that impelled it have not passed by only to leave a trace but remain pent up in the metal, whence they can be released at any time. But here's the rub. The word cannot be made to release its power just by looking *at* it, as one might look at the block capitals of a sign or monument. That is why, were I to ask you to take a look at my object, you would see no word. No amount of hard staring will reveal what it is. But if I ask you to draw it, by tracing either with pencil and paper or in your mind's eye the bends and loops of the metallic strip, then all at once the word will reappear under your hand or before your eyes, like a submarine resurfacing from the sea. The word is truly an Aladdin's lamp: apparently just an inert lump of metal of a curious design, gently stroke it with the eyes and fingers – as Aladdin rubbed the lamp – and whole worlds are unloosed, of vast oceans and empty skies, of warmth and chill, of immense possibility. All it takes is a soft touch – a little gesture, manual or visual – to rekindle the genie of the word and to release an atmosphere.

I can now reveal the identity of my word. It is 'cold', and comes from the following phrase: 'Through Picassos period, the musical Nile, *cold* Scottish sun, warm French sea, and my favourite teeshirt'

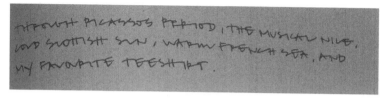

Figure 35 Lines written by Gerry Grams, on the colour 'blue'. From
Shauna McMullan, *Something About a Word* (2011).
(Courtesy of the artist.)

(Figure 35). The phrase was composed by Gerry Grams, one of a
hundred citizens of Bridgeton, in response to a request from Shauna
McMullan to write down what the word *blue* brought to mind. These
handwritten lines were cut out in steel, powder-coated to give a blue-
grey sheen, and suspended in parallel rows aligned on a single vertical
plane (Figure 36). My word is just one sample, kindly donated to me
by the artist, from a much larger composition, and it is time now to
turn to the composition as a whole. In many ways, *Something About
a Word* resembles a polyphonic choral work. Each line has its own
voice, distinguished not only by the particular choice of words, which
give it melody and rhythm, but also by the specific timbre manifest in
the character of the handwriting. Sounding together, however, these
voices create a harmony. Thus the work may be read in the manner of
a musical score, either horizontally (for melody, rhythm and timbre)
or vertically (for harmony), or both ways at once. The relation between
melody and harmony, here, is between line and colour. And that
colour is blue.

There has been a certain tendency among western writers on art to
regard colour as mere embellishment or 'make-up' with the power to
seduce or charm but not, as in drawing or writing, to convey the processes of thought. But there is more to it than that. As a phenomenon
of light, colour lends a particular radiance to things: an atmosphere
or aura that overwhelms the consciousness of those who come under
its spell. Maurice Merleau-Ponty, for example, had this to say about
the blue of the sky: 'I am not set over against it as an acosmic subject;
I do not possess it in thought or spread out towards it some idea of

Figure 36 *Something About a Word,* by Shauna McMullan (2011).
(Courtesy of the artist.)

blue such as might reveal the secret of it. . . . I am the sky itself as it is drawn together and unified . . .; my consciousness is saturated with this limitless blue.'[3] We do not, in short, see light but see *in* the light; since the sky *is* light we see in the sky; since the sky *is* blue we see in its blueness.

Colour, then, is not just an adornment, conferring an outer garb to thought, but the very milieu in which thought occurs. Like the atmosphere with its weather, it gets inside us and makes it so that whatever we do, say or write is done with a certain mood or disposition. It is the temperament of our being. We inhale it as we breathe the air, and on the outward breath of exhalation we weave our lines of speech, song and handwriting into the fabric of the world. Conversely, as we retrace the ways of the hand, crouching in the undulating ribbons of blue-grey steel, so colour is once again released like the genie from the lamp. Line is haptic, colour atmospheric. In the polyphony of *Something About a Word*, the multiple lives, voices and scripts of a community, differentiated in melody, rhythm and timbre, are unified under the harmonic blue of a sky that arches over all.

Au revoir

How should a book end? Physically, it usually ends with a cover, of somewhat thicker material than its pages. Perhaps that's why closing the book feels so very different from turning the page. Inside the book you are like a wanderer, following a trail through a landscape. You can only ever see as far as the next horizon. Yet with every turn, a new horizon opens up before you, while what was a horizon before is now ground underfoot or already receding into the distance. But if that is what it's like to turn the page, there is nothing in the wanderer's experience to compare with closing the cover. For at that moment it is as though the very world itself – a world you had been exploring, and that you had imagined would go on forever – turns its back, revealing itself, after all, to be but a continent, bounded and contained. What had been a gathering of pages morphs into a box with contents. But we inhabit a world, not a box. A box is either open or shut; the fabric of the world, however, is folded. It is never completely open or completely closed. As with life and death, its opening in one place is always a closing in another. There is no shutting it.

This difference between folding and unfolding, on the one hand, and opening and shutting, on the other, is as old as the book. Many centuries before the Christian era, the Etruscans were writing spells and incantations on linen cloth, which would be folded much as we would fold sheets and towels today, while their Greek contemporaries were writing and copying their lemmas on wooden tablets, coated with wax. The Romans inherited both traditions, binding sheets of papyrus or parchment, along the line of the fold, into gatherings, and assembling tablets made from slabs of hardwood, along their edges, into blocks. The first, of a somewhat ephemeral nature, were held about the person and used – much like the notebooks of today

– for casual observations and exercises. The second made up the more durable repositories of law and statute. It is no surprise, then, that both the book (*codex*) and the rules contained therein (*codices*) took their respective names from the Latin for tree-trunk, *caudex*. Ever since Antiquity, the tree and the book have been joined at the trunk.

It was left to the clerics, scholars and craftsmen of the medieval era to combine the two principles, of gathering and assembly, so as to create the book in a form that has persisted into our times. The key to the combination was to treat each multi-page gathering, in effect, as a tablet, and then to bind them together – as the multi-tablet codex had once been bound – between hardwood covers. That's why, in the book, we now find both principles in operation: of folding and unfolding, every time you turn the page, and of opening and shutting, when you lift the front cover at the start, and close the back cover at the end. Not only in the book, however, are the principles of gathering and assembly combined. In a world full of things that have not just grown but have in a sense been shaped, most often by human hands and minds, the assembly and the gathering can no more be prised apart than a thing can be separated from its shadow – or the intellect, for that matter, from the life in which it is sustained.

The intellect is most at home in a world of formal solids, of geometric regularity, where rule, code and theorem hold sway. This is a world in which everything is assembled or joined up, from parts designed to fit with absolute accuracy. But it is also a world of rigid interconnection, with little or no room to breathe, or for the press and stretch of exercise. It is fundamentally inanimate. When it comes to the labour of its formation – to the work and suffering that brought it into being as a crystallization of the fluxes of life and experience – the assembly is silent. Its logic is timeless and eternal. Yet nothing in it actually holds. For things to hold they need to grow tentacles with the flexibility to bend and the sensitivity to respond. They must be able to entwine and clasp like the fingers of two hands. Yet what the hands gather and bind, the intellect divides and partitions. In the modern history of the academy, it has been the mission of the intellect to marshal the data of experience and to box it up within the covers of separate disciplines. Here in the land of academia, where reason is king and the facts stand for themselves, there are no loose ends. Everything is ordered and accounted for. Yet nothing coheres.

Imagine, for example, a wall of bricks. It is held together by the mortar that fills the spaces between them. If the bricks were perfectly fitting, geometric solids, then there should be no intermediate spaces. Yet if there were no spaces to fill, the wall would not stand. The slightest perturbation would bring it crashing down. It is the same with a scale model, assembled from a kit. The parts, moulded or cut in advance, should fit together seamlessly. Yet the modeller also needs glue. Threading through the surfaces over which they are spread – which to the naked eye appear solid but at the atomic level are lattice-like – the long polymeric molecules of glue bind them on contact into a dense weave. And to return to the book, it is the binding of the leaves and covers that prevents it from falling apart in use, despite the handling of readers which tugs at the pages much as the wind, as it blows, tugs at the leaves of trees. The mortar, the glue and the binding threads: these are materials which wind their way around and through the surfaces of the solids they encounter, so as to form a kind of mesh. All, at least to begin with, have properties of fluidity and flexibility. They are the opposite of rigid. But as the mortar eventually hardens, the glue dries and the threads are tied, the mesh tightens, holding the solid components fast in its grip.

The mesh, let us say, is the shadow of the assembly. Abstract the bricks from the wall and you would be left with a continuous, delicate, almost lace-like fabric of mortar. Abstract the parts from the assembled kit and you would have a spidery tangle of adhesive filaments. Abstract the assembled gatherings from the book and you would have a texture of loops, knots and stitches of a kind that would have been familiar to the weaver, basket-maker or embroiderer. Historically, indeed, these were crafts closely allied to bookbinding, and often even practised by the same people, drawing on a common repertoire of techniques. But if it is the weave of the mesh that holds the components of the assembly together, it is also because of the wear and tear, the fraying and eventual breakage of its constituent lines that things fall apart. In a living world, nothing lasts forever, but precisely for this reason, life can carry on indefinitely. Wear and tear holds the promise of renewal.

Do not ask, then, whether this book is an assembly or a gathering. As with everything else of material manufacture, it is both. Like a box, it has contents, and these are the essays assembled herein. Yet every essay is a gathering of sorts, a provisional exercise in observational thinking rather than a conclusive statement of logically interconnected propositions. They are, moreover, held together by lines of correspondence that run through them in just the same way that material threads would have run through the gathered pages, had they been bound using traditional techniques. This dual nature of the book, however, leaves me with a problem. For while my purpose has been to present a gathering of correspondences, modelled on the exchange of letters, the fact that they are assembled into a book introduces moments of opening and closure, marked by the covers, that subvert this very purpose. For opening a letter is not at all like opening a book, nor can a letter – once opened – ever be closed. If it is no longer open, it can only be due to its having been forgotten, discarded or destroyed. Let's pause to compare these operations.

If to open the cover of a book is to lift the lid on its contents, to open a letter is more like opening a door to a visitor. It is to release them from the confinement of their travel and to let them in, over the threshold. In the old days it meant breaking a personalized seal, a ritual not unlike opening a carriage door to welcome an arriving guest. It was customary, after all, to begin the letter with words of greeting, even endearment. Nowadays, if you still exchange letters at all, you would likely take a paperknife to an envelope that the sender has sealed with an adhesive, possibly activated with their own saliva. Either way, the very act of opening is tantamount to a release of lines that had been bottled up, into the continuity of a conversation. The letter is unfolded, flattened out, and the words begin to speak from its pages, as if your correspondent were there in the room, talking to you. And when you've finished? You cannot simply close it again, and restore it to your shelf – as you would return a book to the library – as if it had never been opened. With a box, you can always replace the lid, but the act of breaking a seal or cutting an envelope can never be rescinded.

Since in correspondence, every intervention invites a response, and every response is an intervention in its turn, there is nothing intrinsic to the process that would bring it to a conclusion. As with life itself, the impulse is to carry on. Whereas a book is put away when you have finished, interred within its covers, only neglect or violence can bring an end to correspondence. On the one hand it might simply peter out as letters – buried in a pile of papers or forgotten in a desk drawer – go unanswered. It is not that they would never have called for a response, but as time drags on, and commitment wanes, the call is gradually reduced to a whimper and eventually to silence. On the other hand a correspondence can be terminated abruptly, should a letter either cause offence or place the recipient in a compromising situation, susceptible even to blackmail. In such cases, nothing less than its physical discard or destruction – whether scrunched up and tossed into the bin or consigned to the flames of a fire – can placate the angered or incriminated recipient.

So here's my problem. I do not want our correspondences to end, through either neglect or violence. Yet I am bound to bring this book to a close. And there must come a point when you, too, will close the cover – a point at which you'll say that you have finished it. What then? Will the words stay with you? Of course I hope they do. So let's think of the cover in another way, with less finality. It doesn't have to be about covering *over*, such as when, in the act of burial, the body is covered with a slab. For a cover can also provide shelter and protection, affording safe keeping for future use. Do we not often cover things *in order* to return to them? After all, a book closed can always be reopened, and a good cover will ensure that the pages will not be soiled in the interim. Books can be read, as landscapes can be walked, over and over again. So as you read these words, turn the final page and close the cover, think on the return. As we say on parting, *au revoir*. Since I am writing these lines from my home in Aberdeen, in northeast Scotland, let me sign off with the motto with which this city proudly toasts its visitors: 'Happy to meet, sorry to part, happy to meet again. *Bon Accord!*'

Notes

Preface and acknowledgements

1 Freely available online at *https://knowingfromtheinside.org/*.

Invitation

1 'The crisis of education' (1954), in *Hannah Arendt: Between Past and Future*, introduced by Jerome Kohn, London: Penguin, 2006, pp. 170–93, see p. 193.

2 Tim Ingold, 'Anthropology beyond humanity' (Edward Westermarck Memorial Lecture, May 2013), *Suomen Antropologi* 38(3), 2013: 5–23.

3 Tim Ingold, *The Life of Lines*, Abingdon: Routledge, 2015, pp. 147–53.

4 Amanda Ravetz, 'BLACK GOLD: trustworthiness in artistic research (seen from the sidelines of arts and health)', *Interdisciplinary Science Reviews* 43, 2018: 348–71.

5 Ravetz, 'BLACK GOLD', p. 362.

6 'Digging', in Seamus Heaney, *New Selected Poems, 1966–1987*, London: Faber & Faber, 1990, pp. 1–2.

Somewhere in Northern Karelia . . .

1 *Ground Work: Writings on Places and People*, edited by Tim Dee, London: Jonathan Cape, 2018.

Pitch black and firelight

1 An earlier version of this essay, under the title 'Pitch', was published in *An Unfinished Compendium of Materials*, edited by Rachel Harkness, University of Aberdeen: knowingfromtheinside.org, 2017, pp. 125–6.

2 *Oxford English Dictionary, beam, n.1*, III. 19a.

3 Spike Bucklow, *The Alchemy of Paint: Art, Science and Secrets from the Middle Ages*, London: Marion Boyars, 2009, p. 60.

4 Johann Wolfgang von Goethe, *The Theory of Colours*, translated by Charles Lock Eastlake, London: John Murray, 1840, p. 206, §502.

In the shadow of tree being

1 *In the Shadow of Tree Being: A Walk with Giuseppe Penone* © Tim Ingold; published for the first time in *Giuseppe Penone: The Inner Life of Forms*, edited by Carlos Basualdo, New York: Gagosian, 2018.

Ta, Da, Ça!

1 Roland Barthes, *La chambre claire: Note sur la photographie*, Paris: Gallimard, Le Seuil, 1980, pp. 15–16 (in English: *Camera Lucida: Reflections on Photography*, translated by Richard Howard, Ridgewood, NY: Hill & Wang, 1981, p. 5).

2 See Jean-Pierre Vernant, *Myth and Thought Among the Greeks*, London: Routledge & Kegan Paul, 1983, p. 260.

Spitting, Climbing, Soaring, Falling (Introduction)

1 John Carey, 'Aerial ships and underwater monasteries: the evolution of a monastic marvel', *Proceedings of the Harvard Celtic Colloquium* 12 (1992): 16–28; Seamus Heaney, 'Lightenings', in *New Selected Poems, 1988–2013*, London: Faber & Faber, 2014, p. 32.

2 Saint Augustine, *Confessions*, translated by Henry Chadwick, Oxford: Oxford University Press, 1991, p. 246.

The mountaineer's lament

1 This was the Hielan' Ways Symposium, *Perceptions of Exploration*, 14–15 November 2014, Tomintoul, Moray.
2 Alfred North Whitehead, *The Concept of Nature* (The Tarner Lectures, 1919), Cambridge: Cambridge University Press, 1964, pp. 14–15.

On flight

1 *Aerocene*, edited and coordinated by Studio Tomás Saraceno, Milan: Skira Editore, 2017.
2 On dreams of flying, see Gaston Bachelard, *Air and Dreams: An Essay on the Imagination of Movement*, translated by Edith and Frederick Farrell, Dallas, TX: Dallas Institute Publications, 1988, pp. 65–89.
3 This is a quotation from the Tate Gallery display caption. See *http://www.tate.org.uk/art/artworks/lanyon-thermal-t00375*.
4 Titus Lucretius Carus, *On the Nature of Things* [*De Rerum Natura*], translated by William Ellery Leonard, New York: Dutton, 1921, p. 38.
5 Henri Bergson, *Creative Evolution*, translated by Arthur Mitchell, New York: Henry Holt, 1911, p. 128.

Sounds of snow

1 Mikel Nieto, *A Soft Hiss of This World*, 2019, see *http://mikelrnieto.net/en/publications/books/a-soft-hiss/*.
2 The theologian John Hull, who became blind in mid-life, describes how steadily falling rain 'has a way of bringing out the contours of everything'. See John Hull, *On Sight and Insight: A Journey into the World of Blindness*, Oxford: Oneworld Publications, 1997, p. 26.
3 For these and other references to Scots terms, I am indebted to Amanda Thomson, *A Scots Dictionary of Nature*, Glasgow: Saraband, 2018.

Going to Ground (Introduction)

1 Edwin Abbott, *Flatland: A Romance of Many Dimensions*, London: Seeley & Co., 1884.

Scissors paper stone

1 Paul Klee, *Notebooks, Volume 1: The Thinking Eye*, edited by Jürg Spiller, translated by Ralph Manheim, London: Lund Humphries, 1961, p. 105.

2 Tom Brown, Jr, *The Tracker: The True Story of Tom Brown, Jr, as Told to William Jon Watkins*, New York: Prentice Hall, 1978, p. 6.

3 John Ruskin, *The Works of John Ruskin* (Library Edition), Volume 7, edited by Edward Tyas Cook and Alexander Wedderburn, London: George Allen, 1905, pp. 14–15.

Ad coelum

1 'Volumetric sovereignty: a forum', edited by Franck Billé, *Society + Space*, 2019; full collection available at *http://www.societyandspace. org/forums/volumetric-sovereignty*.

Are we afloat?

1 See *http://www.arts-et-metiers.net/musee/paris-flotte-t-il*.

Shelter

1 Tim Knowles, *The Howff Project*, Bristol: Intellect, 2019.

Doing time

1 *LA+ International Journal of Landscape Architecture* no. 8, special issue 'Time', edited by Richard Weller and Tatum L. Hands, University of Pennsylvania School of Design, 2018.

2 Adrian Heathfield and Tehching Hsieh, *Out of Now: The Lifeworks of Tehching Hsieh*, London: Live Art Development Agency; Cambridge, MA: MIT Press, 2009.
3 Heathfield and Hsieh, *Out of Now*, pp. 327, 334.

The Ages of the Earth (Introduction)

1 Julie Cruikshank, 2005, *Do Glaciers Listen? Local Knowledge, Colonial Encounters and Social Imagination*, Vancouver: UBC Press; Seattle: University of Washington Press.

The elements of fortune

1 *YOU: Collection Lafayette Anticipations*, Paris: Musée d'Art moderne de Paris, 2019.
2 Lucretius, *The Nature of Things*, translated by A. E. Stallings, introduced by Richard Jenkyns, London: Penguin, 2007, p. 42.

A stone's life

1 *Être pierre: Catalogue de l'exposition au musée Zadkine*, Paris: Paris Musées, 2017.
2 The weight of bodies, according to philosopher Jean-Luc Nancy, 'is the raising of their masses to the surface'. Jean-Luc Nancy, *Corpus*, translated by Richard Rand, New York: Fordham University Press, 2008, p. 93.

The jetty

1 *Catalyst: Art, Sustainability and Place in the Work of Wolfgang Weileder*, edited by Simon Guy, Bielefeld: Kerber Verlag, 2015.

On extinction

1 Originally published by Little Toller Books in *The Clearing*, 29 November 2018, available at *https://www.littletoller.co.uk/the-clearing/on-extinction-by-tim-ingold/*.

Three short fables of reinforcement

1 Walter Behrmann, 'Der Vorgang der Selbstverstärkung' [The Process of Self-Reinforcement], *Zeitschrift der Gesellschaft für Erdkunde zu Berlin*, 1919: 153–7.

2 *Grain, Vapor, Ray: Textures of the Anthropocene (Volume 1, Grain)*, edited by Katrin Klingan, Ashkan Sepahvand, Christoph Rosol and Bernd M. Scherer, Cambridge, MA: MIT Press, 2015, pp. 137–46. Reprinted in *The End of the World Project*, edited by Richard Lopez, John Bloomberg-Rissman and T. C. Marshall, Munster, IN: Moria Books, 2019, pp. 546–55.

Lines in the landscape

1 Cited in Edward Laning, *The Art of Drawing*, New York: McGraw Hill, 1971, p. 32.

Fold

1 *TALWEG 01*, Strasbourg: Pétrole Éditions, 2014, see *http://www.petrole-editions.com/editions/talweg01*.

Taking a thread for a walk

1 First published in Anne Masson and Eric Chevalier, *des choses à faire*, Gent: MER, 2015, pp. 71–9.

2 Tim Ingold, *Lines: A Brief History*, Abingdon: Routledge, 2007, pp. 69–70.

Letter-line and strike-through

1 The video was created by Anna Macdonald in 2016 as part of a joint research project with Marie-Andrée Jacob, University of Keele, and funded by a Fellowship from the Arts and Humanities Research Council (grant number AH/J008338/1). See Marie-Andrée Jacob, 'The strikethrough: an approach to regulatory writing and professional discipline', *Legal Studies* 37/1, 2017: 137–61; Marie-Andrée Jacob and Anna Macdonald, 'A change of heart: retraction and body', *Law Text Culture* 23, 2019, special issue, 'Legal Materiality', edited by Hyo Yoon Kang and Sara Kendall.

2 Raphael Rubinstein, 'Missing: ~~erasure~~ | Must include: erasure', in *UNDER ~~ERASURE~~*, curated by Heather + Raphael Rubinstein, Pierogi Gallery, New York, published by Nonprofessional Experiments, 2018–19, *http://www.under-erasure.com*.

3 This idea is discussed at length by Gayatri Chakravorty Spivak, in her translator's introduction to Jacques Derrida, *Of Grammatology*, Baltimore, MD: Johns Hopkins University Press, 1974, pp. ix–lxxxvii.

4 The book, with illustrations by Audubon, was published in London and Edinburgh between 1827 and 1838.

5 As in the title of Raphael Rubinstein's essay 'Missing: ~~erasure~~ | Must include: erasure', cited above.

For the Love of Words (Introduction)

1 Maurice Merleau-Ponty, *Phenomenology of Perception*, translated by Colin Smith, London: Routledge & Kegan Paul, 1962, p. 187.

Words to meet the world

1 *Non-Representational Methodologies: Re-Envisioning Research*, edited by Philip Vannini, Abingdon: Routledge, 2015.

In defence of handwriting

1 *Writing Across Boundaries*, Department of Anthropology, Durham University, *https://www.dur.ac.uk/writingacrossboundaries/*.

Diabolism and logophilia

1 Kenneth R. Olwig, *The Meanings of Landscape: Essays on Place, Space, Environment and Justice*, Abingdon: Routledge, 2019.

2 The list, from 2014, is entitled 'Ministry of Defence acronyms and abbreviations', and is available at *https://www.gov.uk/govern ment/publications/ministry-of-defence-acronyms-and-abbreviations*. Strictly speaking, acronyms are distinguished from abbreviations on the grounds of whether they are pronounced as a word (thus SAM as 'sam') or by voicing their constituent letters (thus UDV as 'youdeevee'). Here, however, I adopt a more inclusive definition of the acronym to cover any abbreviation composed of initial letters, regardless of how it is pronounced.

3 Yi-Fu Tuan, *Topophilia: A Study of Environmental Perceptions, Attitudes, and Values*, Englewood Cliffs, NJ: Prentice-Hall, 1974.

Cold blue steel

1 Shauna McMullan, *Something About a Word*, Glasgow: Graphical House, 2011.

2 Claude Lévi-Strauss, *Tristes tropiques*, translated by John and Doreen Weightman, London: Jonathan Cape, 1955, p. 299.

3 Maurice Merleau-Ponty, *Phenomenology of Perception*, translated by Colin Smith, London: Routledge & Kegan Paul, 1962, p. 214.